BEADED BAGS & A

edited by Jules & Kaethe Klio

The beaded bag, today's popular accessory, saw its full development in the 1920s when the knitted, crocheted or woven beaded bag was a necessity for both formal and informal wear. The bag could be embellished with any of the many ornate frames then available, or they could be without frame and maintained with a simple draw string closure of beads, chain or cord.

This volume includes a selection of popular instruction books of this period, illustrating the rich designs popular during this period. Where charted, the patterns can be used for knitting, crocheting or weaving. Realizing that none of the illustrated frames are available today as catalog items, many similar frames can be found through antique and collectable outlets. It is also possible to adapt many of these patterns to frames which are readily available, some of which are illustrated on page 100.

The designs from *A CHARMING COLLECTION OF MODERN BEADED BAGS* have been reproduced from a less then perfect original and, in some cases, lines of instruction are missing. All bags have been included for their historical interest.

Source material for this publication consists of:

THE BOOK OF BAGS NO. 2, Heminway Silks, 1924.
ELIZABETH BEAD WORK BOOK, FIRST EDITION, Elizabeth S. Kay, E.S. Kay, 1922
A CHARMING COLLECTION OF MODERN BEADED BAGS, Dritz-Traum Co., 1924
VIRGINIA SNOW'S AUTHORITY ON BEAD BAGS, NECKLACES, ETC. BOOK NO, 29, Collingbourne's 1926
WELDON'S PRACTICAL BEAD-WORK, c. 1890

Materials

Referenced knitting needle sizes are designated differently today, old and new designations as follows:

#15	000 or 3-0
#16	0000 or 4-0
#17	00000 or 5-0
#18	000000 or 6-0
#19	00000000 or 8-0

THREADS

While silk was the preferred thread for beading, varieties of nylon and cotton, now available can also be used. Some suggested threads:

Gudebrod Silk: A tight work Available from fin ____ (____y), 0 (600y), A (475y), B (390y), C (310y), D (260y), E (200y), F (140y), FF (115y). White or black, also in colors in sizes E, F, FF. Size "E" suggested for most beading applications.

"Hy-Mark" Cotton: A fine cotton thread, similar to a #30 cotton, with a glace or coated finish and extremely strong. A preferred thread for bead work.

Gudebrod Nylon: A strong, tight twisted 3-ply bonded thread which will not naturally untwist or split. Recommended for bead work. Available in white, black, natural and beige in sizes #C and #B.

BEADS

Prestrung beads preferred. Size #11 most common. Available in both matte and gloss finish in a wide range of colors. Beads are strung in hanks of approximately 4100 beads (19 beads measure 1") ready to be transferred to your working thread. It is always suggested that you work up a few rows and compare with pattern size.

Contents

Note: Numbers in [ ] designate page numbers of this book, Other page references are from the original publications and are retained for text continuity.

LACIS
PUBLICATIONS
3163 Adeline Street, Berkeley, CA 94703

© 1998, LACIS
ISBN 1-891656-02-3

The
BOOK *of* BAGS
No. 2

PRICE 10¢

HEMINWAY SILKS

MADE IN U.S.A.

Crochet *and* Knitting Stitches

Abbreviations

S.—Silk,	P.—Picot.	Sl. St.—Slip Stitch.
Sk.—Skip.	R.—Ridge.	S. C.—Single Crochet.
Sp.—Space.	Kn.—Knit.	D. C.—Double Crochet.
L.—Loop.	Ch.—Chain.	H. D. C.—Half Double Crochet.
M.—Mesh.	St.—Stitch.	T. C. or Tr. C.—Treble Crochet.
R.—Ring.	Inc.—Increase.	D. Tr. C.—Double Treble Crochet.
P.—Purl.	Dec.—Decrease.	*—Repetition.

Chain Stitch—To begin the ch., form the first loop and insert the hook, then * throw the thread over the hook, and draw a loop through the loop on the hook, thus forming 1 ch. st.; repeat from * as often as desired.

Slip Stitch—Begin with a length of ch.

Skip 1 ch., * insert the hook into the next ch., throw the thread over the hook, and draw a loop through the st. and the loop on the hook, repeat from * to end of row. Sl. st. is mostly used to close a row or round, or to join 2 motifs together.

Single Crochet—Make a ch. for the length required.

Skip 1 ch., * insert the hook into the next ch., throw the thread over, and draw a loop through the st., throw thread over, and draw through the 2 loops on the hook; repeat from * to the end of row.

Single crochet stitches worked back and forth taken up on the back thread only form a rib and is often called slipper st.

Half Double Crochet—Make a ch. for the desired length.

1st Row—Skip 2 ch., * throw the thread over and insert the hook into the next ch., throw the thread over and draw a loop through, throw the thread over, and draw through the 3 loops on the hook; repeat from * to end of row.

Double Crochet—Make a ch. for the length desired.

Skip 3 ch., * throw the thread over and insert the hook into the next ch., throw the thread over and draw a loop through, thread over, through 2 loops, thread over, through 2 loops; repeat from * to the end of row.

Treble Crochet—Make a ch. of the length desired.

Skip 4 ch., * throw the thread over twice, insert the hook into the next ch., throw the thread over and draw a loop through, thread over, through 2 loops, thread over, through 2 loops, thread over, through 2 loops; repeat from * to end of row.

Double Treble—Make a ch. for the required length.

Skip 5 ch., * throw thread over 3 times, insert the hook into the next ch., throw the thread over, and draw a loop through, thread over, through 2 loops, thread over, through 2 loops, thread over, through 2 loops, thread over, through 2 loops; repeat from * to the end of row.

Picot—4 ch., and 1 s. c. into the first ch. to form a p.

Simplifying *the* Manner *of* Crocheting *and* Knitting *with* Beads

Stringing of Beads: Loosen 1 string of bunch of beads: if silk thread is heavy take a pair of scissors and file off until a finer thread is secured, then place silk over bead thread and make one single turn and draw cotton through loop with crochet needle: another way is to thread fine needle with silk and draw through cotton thread, hold threads back with left hand pushing beads over on silk thread very carefully.

Crocheting With Beads: Thread one bunch of beads on to spool of silk. If beads are not used in very beginning of bag, push back on unwinding silk thread until needed. Insert needle in stitch of previous row, pull loop through, push bead toward needle, silk over needle, pull through both loops on needle, needle in next st., continue around. All beaded bags are worked from the inside, this throws the beads to front or right side of bag. Some complete by taking up the back of stitch only, which makes a finer, more finished looking stitch, and still others work through the entire stitch, which makes a stronger, firmer bag.

Knitting With Beads: Thread one bunch of beads on to spool of silk. Insert needle in st., push bead toward needle, complete or knit the st., continue around. To knit round bags, insert needle in back of st., push bead toward needle, pull bead through st. along with silk, continue around.

Directions *for* Washing Heminway Pure Silk Articles

Dip the article in tepid or cold water and let it lie a few moments. Press out water and place again in very warm Ivory soap suds, pressing between hands to clean. It may be necessary to rub gently to remove deeper stains. Rinse twice in tepid or cold water; lay in folds of Turkish towel until moisture is absorbed and nearly dry; if necessary, press with medium hot iron between dry towels.

No. 600

The BIARRITZ No. 600

Knitted Bag with Blue Silk Background. Spanish Butterfly and Bee Design in Steel Beads.

Made with HEMINWAY SILKS

Materials: No. 666 Navy, 2 spools Purse Twist, 9 bunches Steel Beads No. 8 or 9, ¼ yd. Silk or Satin for lining, 6 Brass Rings (½ inch diameter), 1 pair No. 18 Steel Knitting Needles.

Border at Top of Bag: String 3 bunches of Steel Beads (B.) on 1 spool of silk, cast on 89 sts. Knit (kn.) 3 rows plain. **Throughout the design there is** always a return row of plain knitting, this will not be mentioned again. As per diagram there is always 1 kn. st. on each side of bag. **4th row.**—Kn. 2 sts., * insert needle in next st., push a B. toward needle, kn. or complete the st., kn. 1, * repeat across row, end kn. 2 sts. **5th row.**—Kn. 1 st.

Concluded on page 7

89 stitches across - 106 ridges in length

Biarritz Bag No. 600   Background in navy silk-design in steel beads.

No. 614

The BROOKLAWN No. 614

Lovely Summer Bag—Dainty Enough to Accompany the Frock of the Graduate or Debutante.

Made with HEMINWAY SILKS

Materials: No. 4 Cream, 2 spools Purse Twist; 15 bunches Glass Beads, Soft Green or any shade desired; ¼ yard Cream or Green Satin for lining; 1 Steel Crochet Needle No. 11.

Bottom of Bag: Ch. 5, join in ring (R.).

1st row.—8 s. c. in R. (size—7½ in. long, 7½ in. wide at centre, 5¼ in. at top). **2nd row.**—Ch. 1, s. c. with bead (B.) in 1st st., * ch. 1, s. c. in next st. * repeat around (the st. used in bottom of bag is s. c. with always 1 ch. between). **3rd row.**—Ch. 1, s. c. with B. on 1st s. c., 3 more s. c. with B. on next 3 s. c., * s. c. with B. on next ch, 1 for inc. (all inc. is done on "ch. 1"), 4 s. c. with B. on next 4 s. c. * continue around. 20 more rows inc. at irregular points in rows as necessary to keep the work in "saucer" shape, 6 more rows without inc., on the last row there are about 124 s. c. with B. 2 more rows of plain s. c., inc. to 180 sts. (by work s. c. on "ch. 1" at irregular points in 2 rows) so that 2 inc. do not occur directly over each other.

Inverted Pyramid Border: Work out design as shown in diagram No. 1. There should be 15 sections, allowing 12 sts. to each section, continue diagram, x represents green beads. 3 more rows without B.

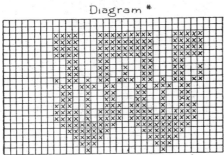

Diagram *

The Brooklawn No 614
Crocheted Bag

There are 15 designs around bag

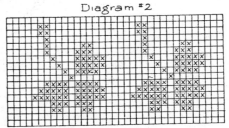

Diagram #2

There are eleven leaves of clover around top of bag

Bullion at Center of Bag: Ch. 5 (which counts 1 tr. c.), 1 tr. c. on ch., * insert needle in next st., pull up long loop (L.) long as tr. c. just made, push 5 B. toward needle, silk over needle, pull silk through all L. on needle, ch. 1 tightly, 2 tr. c. in next 2 sts., * repeat around ending row with 5 B. (60 beaded bullion loops in row). **2nd row.**—Ch. 5, * insert needle between 1st 2 tr. c. of previous row for beaded bullion loop, 1 tr. c. on beaded bullion loop of previous row * repeat around, ending with 1 tr. c. Alternate the 1st and 2nd rows 7 times more, 16 rows in all. 1 row of plain s. c. skipping ch. 1. 3 more rows s. c. on s. c.

Clover Border: Continue as per diagram No. 2, finish bag with 1 row plain s. c.

Beading: Ch. 5, 3 tr. c. in next 3 sts., * ch. 4, sk. 4, 4 tr. c. in next 4 sts. * repeat around top of bag having 24 tr. c. groups.

Picot Finish: * 2 s. c. on 1st 2 tr. c., ch. 4, sl. st. in 1st ch., ch. 5, sl. st. in same st., ch. 4, sl. st. in same st., 2 s. c. in next 2 tr. c., 3 s. c. over ch. 4, * repeat around top of bag, break silk.

Cords: Using 3 strands of silk, ch. 1 loosely, * silk over needle, insert needle in ch. 1, pull L. through, silk over, pull through all L. on needle, * repeat to 24 inch length for each cord, draw through beading from opposite side of bag and close neatly. Cut satin lining shape of completed bag, sew up sides of lining, place in bag and sl. st. to bag just below beading.

The BIARRITZ No. 600

Concluded from page 5

without B., kn. 1 with B., continue across. **6th row.**—Same as 4th row. **7th row.**—Same as 5th row. **8th row.**—Same as 6th row. **9th and 10th rows.**—Plain kn. (Size of bag, 6¾ in. by 8 in.) **11th, 12th and 13th rows.**—Kn. 1, kn. 4 sts. with B., * kn. 2 sts. without B., kn. 5 with B., repeat * to *. Design begins on 14th row from top of bag, continue working as per diagram until design is complete, then 2 rows plain kn., complete bottom same as top border. This finishes ½ of bag. Make a 2nd half. Care must be taken to keep of same width and length throughout. It may be necessary to stretch the 2 pieces overnight, by pinning to some soft thick material with right side downward, then set warm iron on (do not rub iron over kn.), remove and sew up sides and bottom, make a crinolin pocket of same size, slip into bag before lining with silk or satin, sl. st. around top neatly. Cover 6 rings in s. c. and sew ¾ inch from top at even distances apart.

Cord: Using 6 threads make 2 chains each 20 inches long, run through rings from each side of bag and join with fancy knot.

Bead Fringe: Attach silk on corner of bag, string with B. needle 4 inches of B., fasten ¼ inch on bottom of bag, string another 4 inches, wind twice through L. just made, continue across winding twice each time through L. (20 L. in all).

No. 601

The BRAE BURN No. 601

*A Magical Bag of Chinese Coloring, and most unusual as
its beauty lies in the varied shading, from dark to light at top,
of its silk background with one color only of beads for design.*

Made with HEMINWAY SILKS

Materials: Nos. 2249 Dk. Brown, 2032 Henna, 2285 Tangerine, 821 Lt. Brown, 2000 Gold, 4 or 5 Cream, 1 spool each Hampton or Concord Crochet Silk, 12 bunches Peach Beads; 1 Ring, 1 inch diameter; 2 Steel Crochet Needles, Nos. 11 and 4.

Bottom of Four Sided Bag: String 2 bunches of beads (B.) on Dk. Brown silk No. 2249, ch. 5, join in ring (R.). **1st row.**—12 s. c. in R. (work round and round). **2nd row.**—* 1 s. c. with B. in 1st s. c., 1 s. c. without B. in same st., 1 s. c. without B. in next st., 1 s. c. with B. in same st., 1 s. c. with B. in next st. * repeat around 3 times more, over the 3 sections. **3rd row.**—* 1 s. c. with B. on B. of previous row, 1 s. c. with B. on next st., 1 s. c. without B. in same st., 1 s. c. without B. in next st., 1 s. c. with B. in same st., 1 s. c. with B. in next 2 sts. * repeat 3 times more. 12 more

Concluded on page 21

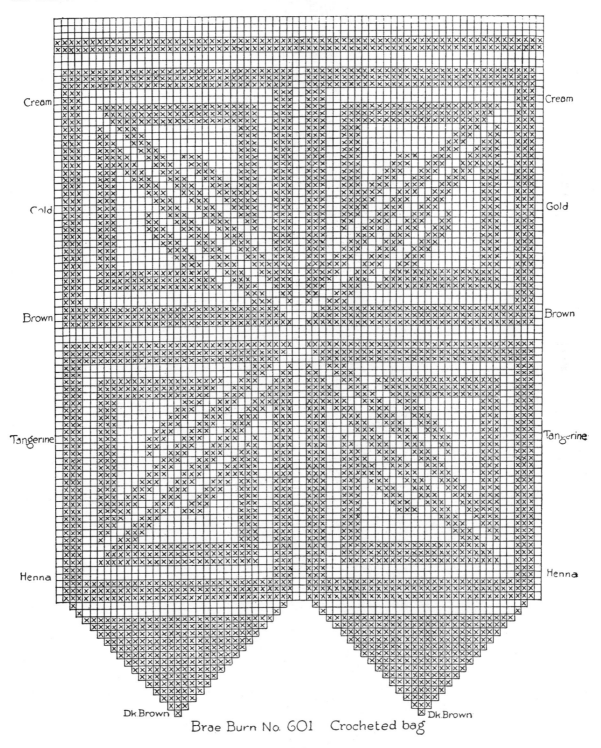

Cream

Gold

Brown

Tangerine

Henna

Dk. Brown

Brae Burn No. 601   Crocheted bag

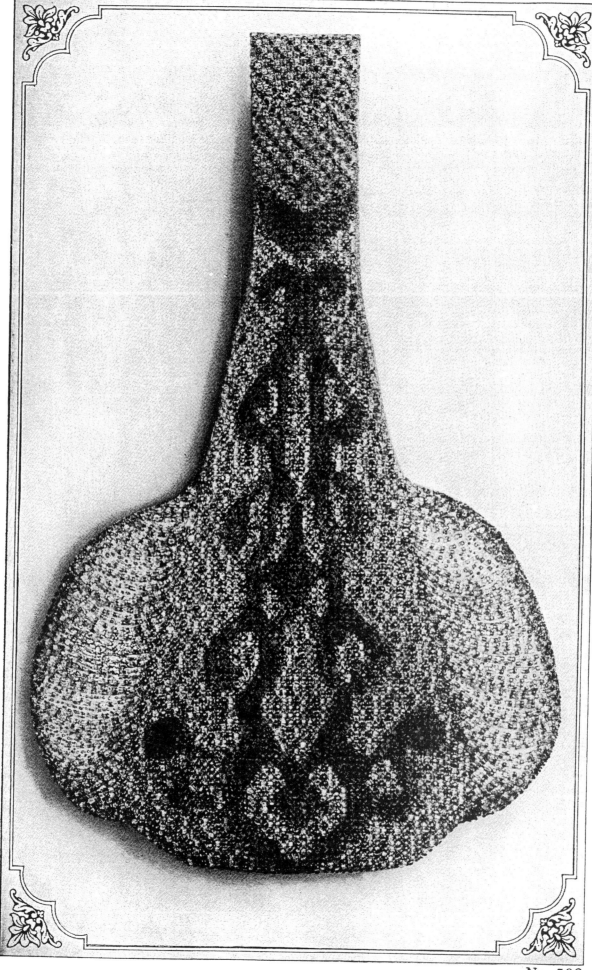

No. 598

SOU LE BRAS PAISLEY BAG No. 598

This most unusual little bag worn Sou le bras is shown in Paisley colorings. Lovely bags with Persian, Indian or Chinese design may be equally as effective in the same shape, using their native colorings in silk and beads.

Made with HEMINWAY SILKS

Materials: No. 3557 Bronze Brown, or Nos. 3512 Tan, 2000 Gold, 830 Gray, 2 spools of Purse Twist; 9 bunches Green Beads, 9 bunches Red Beads, 9 bunches Yellow Beads, 5 bunches Navy Blue Beads; 1 pair No. 16 Steel Knitting Needles; 1 Steel Crochet Needle No. 10.

Note: Slip the first st. of every row. Entire bag is knitted with one bead (b.) between each st. Thread beads for Paisley background according to diagram in following order always, green, yellow red; green, yellow, red; stringing in blue beads for the design as directed, following text matter. On 1 spool of silk string b. from 1st to 220th row inclusive and on next spool 219th to 1st row inclusive.

Cast on 36 sts. (Paisley Beads, P.; Blue Beads, Bl.).

1st and 2nd rows.—35 P. B. **3rd row.**—Inc. 1 st., 17 P., 1 Bl., 17 P. **4th row.**—Inc. 1 st., 36 P. **5th row.**—Inc. 1 st., 17 P., 3 Bl., 17 P. **6th row.**— Inc. 1 st., 38 P. **7th row.**—Inc. 1 st., 17 P., 5 Bl., 17 P. **8th row.**—Inc. 1 st., 40 P. **9th row.**— Inc. 1 st., 17 P., 3 Bl., 1 P., 3 Bl., 17 P. **10th row.**—Inc. 1 st., 42 P. **11th row.**—Inc. 1 st., 16 P., 4 Bl., 3 P., 4 Bl., 16 P. **12th row.**—Inc. 1 st., 44 P. **13th row.**—Inc. 1 st., 16 P., 4 Bl., 5 P., 4 Bl., 16 P. **14th row.**—Inc. 1 st., 46 P. **15th row.**—Inc. 1 st., 16 P., 4 Bl., 7 P., 4 Bl., 16 P. **16th row.**—Inc. 1 st., 48 P. **17th row.**— Inc. 1 st., 15 P., 6 Bl., 7 P., 6 Bl., 15 P. **18th row.**—Inc. 1 st., 50 P. **19th row.**—Inc. 1 st., 15 P., 5 Bl., 5 P., 1 Bl., 5 P., 5 Bl., 15 P. **20th row.**—Inc. 1 st., 52 P. **21st row.**—Inc. 1 st., 16 P., 4 Bl., 5 P., 3 Bl., 5 P., 4 Bl., 16 P. **22nd row.**—Inc. 1 st., 54 P. **23rd row.**—Inc. 1 st., 11 P., 3 Bl., 2 P., 4 Bl., 5 P., 5 Bl., 5 P., 4 Bl., 2 P., 3 Bl., 11 P. **24th row.**—Inc. 1 st., 56 P. **25th row.**—Inc. 1 st., 11 P., 5 Bl., 1 P., 4 Bl., 3 P., 3 Bl., 3 P., 3 Bl., 3 P., 4 Bl., 1 P., 5 Bl., 11 P. **26th row.**—Inc. 1 st., 58 P. **27th row.**—Loop (L.) of 10 P., Knit (kn.) 10 P., 6 Bl., 1 P., 4 Bl., 3 P., 3 Bl., 3 P., 3 Bl., 3 P., 4 Bl., 1 P., 6 Bl., 10 P. **28th row.**— L. 10 P., kn. 57 P. **29th row.**—L. of 14 P., kn. 10 P., 5 Bl., 2 P., 4 Bl., 4 P., 3 Bl., 1 P., 3 Bl., 4 P., 4 Bl., 2 P., 5 Bl., 10 P. **30th row.**— L. 14 P., kn. 57 P. **31st row.**— L. 18 P., dec. 1, kn. 9 P., 2 Bl. 6 P., 3 Bl., 5 P., 5 Bl., 5 P., 3 Bl., 6 P., 2 Bl., 9 P., dec. 1. **32nd row.**—L. 18 P., kn. 55 P. **33rd row.**—L. 22 P., kn. 9 P., 2 Bl., 6 P., 3 Bl., 7 P., 1 Bl., 7 P., 3 Bl., 6 P., 2 Bl., 9 P. **34th row.**—L. 22 P., kn. 55 P. **35th row.**—L. 26 P., kn. 9 P., 2 Bl., 6 P., 4 Bl., 5 P., 3 Bl., 5 P., 4 Bl., 6 P., 2 Bl., 9 P. **36th row.**—L. 26 P., kn. 55 P. **37th row.**— L. 30 P., dec. 1, kn. 9 P., 1 Bl., 5 P., 6 Bl., 3 P., 5 Bl., 3 P., 6 Bl., 5 P., 1 Bl., 9 P., dec. 1. **38th row.**—L. 30 P., kn. 53 P. **39th row.** —L. 34 P., kn. 10 P., 2 Bl., 2 P., 8 Bl., 1 P., 2 Bl., 3 P., 2 Bl., 1 P., 8 Bl., 2 P., 2 Bl., 10 P. **40th row.**—L. 34 P..

Continued on page 13

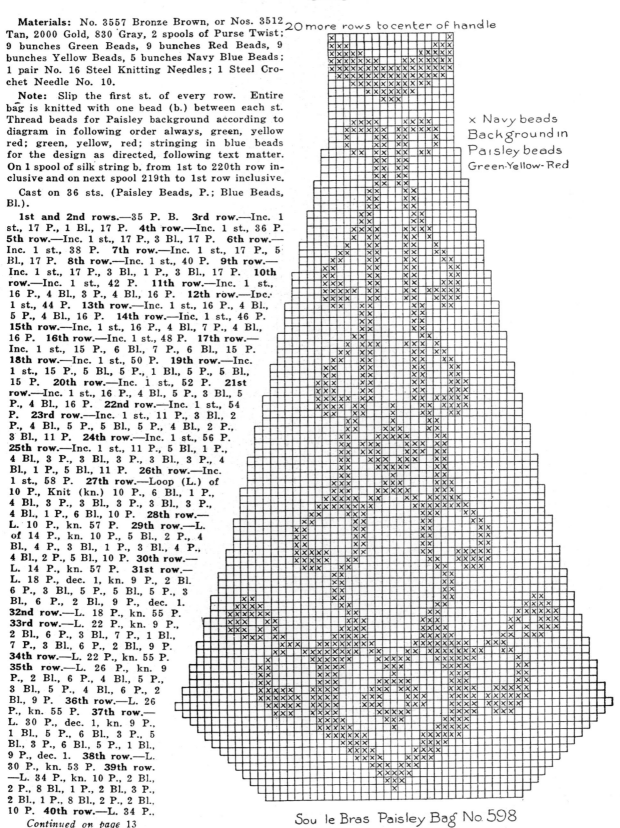

20 more rows to center of handle

x Navy beads
Background in
Paisley beads
Green-Yellow-Red

Sou le Bras Paisley Bag No. 598

The DIGBY No. 609

Round Knitted Bag showing Ridges of Steel Beads.

Made with HEMINWAY SILKS

Materials: No. 666 or 665 Navy Blue, or Nos. 68 Red, 832 Grey, 2 spools Purse Twist; 15 bunches Steel Beads No. 8; 1 round Mold (½ inch diameter); ¼ yd. Navy Satin for lining; 4 Steel Knitting Needles No. 18.

Cast on 36 sts. on each of 3 needles (108 sts. in all). Knit (kn.) 2 rows plain. Kn. 3 sts., sl. 2 beads (B.), kn. 3 sts., sl. 2 B., repeat for 2 rows. Kn. 3 sts., sl. 4 B., repeat for 2 rows. Kn. 3 sts., sl. 6 B., repeat for 2 rows. Kn. 3 sts., slip 10 B., repeat for 2 rows. Kn. 3 sts., sl. 8 B., dec. B. back again to 2 B. Make 4 rows of 2 B. Complete 3 of these patterns. Make 2 patterns inc. to 8 B. Make 1 pattern of 6 B. Kn. 2 sts. together, between each group of B., make 1 pattern of 4 B., kn. 2 sts. together (making 1 st. between B.), kn. 1 st., sl. 2 B., sl. 2 B. for 2 rows, then kn. 1 st., sl. 1 B., repeat once, kn. 2 sts. together, sl. 1 B., repeat until narrowed down to 8 sts., bind off.

Top: 1 row of s. c. in each knitted st., 2 more rows s c., dec. 8 sts. at different points.

Band Loops: * 5 s. c. with B. in each s. c. **2nd row.**—Ch. 1, s. c. on s. c. without B. **3rd row.**—Ch. 1, 5 s. c. with B. on s. c., repeat 2nd and 3rd rows for 2 inches, fold back and sl. st. to top of bag, ch. 5, sl. st. through opposite corner of band and top of bag, sl. st. over 8 s. c. to next L., * repeat 7 times more.

SOU LE BRAS PAISLEY BAG No. 598

Continued from page 11

kn. 53 P. **41st row.**—L. 38 P., kn. 11 P., 3 Bl., 2 P., 8 Bl., 5 P., 8 Bl., 2 P., 3 Bl., 11 P. **42nd row.**—L. 38 P., kn. 53 P. **43rd row.**—L. 42 P., dec. 1, kn. 5 P., 3 Bl., 1 P., 2 Bl., 6 P., 5 Bl., 7 P., 5 Bl., 6 P., 2 Bl., 1 P., 3 Bl., 5 P., dec. 1. **44th row.**—L. 42 P., kn. 51 P. **45th row.**—L. 46 P., kn. 3 P., 3 Bl., 1 P., 1 Bl., 1 P., 1 Bl., 8 P., 4 Bl., 7 P., 4 Bl., 8 P., 1 Bl., 1 P., 1 Bl., 1 P., 3 Bl., 3 P. **46th row.**—L. 46 P., kn. 51 P. **47th row.**—L. 50 P., kn. 3 P., 3 Bl., 2 P., 2 Bl., 9 P., 3 Bl., 7 P., 3 Bl., 9 P., 2 Bl., 3 Bl., 3 P. **48th row.**—L. 50 P., kn. 51 P. **49th row.**—L. 54 P., dec. 1, kn. 2 P., 6 Bl., 10 P., 2 Bl., 9 P., 2 Bl., 10 P., 6 Bl., 2 P., dec. 1. **50th row.**—L. 54 P., kn. 49 P. **51st row.**—L. 58 P., kn. 3 P., 4 Bl., 10 P., 2 Bl., 11 P., 2 Bl., 10 P., 4 Bl., 3 P. **52nd row.**—L. 58 P., kn. 49 P. **53rd row.**—L. 60 P., kn. 4 P., 2 Bl., 10 P., 2 Bl., 13 P., 2 Bl., 10 P., 2 Bl., 4 P. **54th row.**—L. 60 P., kn. 49 P. **55th row.**—L. 60 P., dec. 1, kn. 15 P., 2 Bl., 13 P., 2 Bl., 15 P., dec. 1. **56th row.**—L. 60 P., kn. 47 P. **57th row.**—L. 60 P., kn. 15 P., 2 Bl., 13 P., 2 Bl., 15 P. **58th row.**—L. 60 P., kn. 47 P. **59th row.**—L. 60 P., kn. 15 P., 2 Bl., 13 P., 2 Bl., 15 P. **60th row.**—Same as 58th row. **61st row.**—L. 60 P., dec. 1, kn. 10 P., 3 Bl., 2 P., 2 Bl., 11 P., 2 Bl., 2 P., 3 Bl., 10 P., dec. 1. **62nd row.**—L. 60 P., kn. 45 P. **63rd row.**—L. 60 P., kn. 9 P., 5 Bl., 2 P., 2 Bl., 9 P., 2 Bl., 2 P., 5 Bl., 9 P. **64th row.**—Same as 62nd row. **65th row.**—L. 60 P., kn. 9 P., 5 Bl., 3 P., 2 Bl., 7 P., 2 Bl., 3 P., 5 Bl., 9 P. **66th row.**—Same as 62nd row. **67th row.**—L. 60 P., dec. 1, kn. 8 P., 2 Bl., 6 P., 2 Bl., 7 P., 2 Bl., 6 P., 2 Bl., 8 P., dec. 1. **68th row.**—L. 60 P., kn. 43 P. **69th row.**—L. 60 P., kn. 8 P., 2 Bl., 6 P., 2 Bl., 7 P., 2 Bl., 6 P., 2 Bl., 8 P. **70th row.**—Same as 68th row. **71st row.**—Same as 69th row. **72nd row.**—Same as 68th row. **73rd row.**—L. 60 P., kn. 9 P., 2 Bl., 5 P., 2 Bl., 7 P., 2 Bl., 5 P., 2 Bl., 9 P. **74th row.**—Same as 68th row. **75th row.**—L. 60 P., dec. 1, kn. 9 P., 2 Bl., 3 Bl., 7 P., 3 Bl., 3 P., 2 Bl., 9 P., dec. 1. **76th row.**—L. 60 P., kn 41 P. **77th row.**—L. 60 P., kn. 10 P., 8 Bl., 5 P., 8 Bl., 10 P. **78th row.**—Same as 76th row. **79th row.**—L. 60 P., kn. 11 P., 5 Bl., 1 P., 2 Bl., 3 P., 2 Bl., 1 P., 5 Bl., 11 P. **80th row.**—Same as 76th row. **81st row.**—L. 60 P., kn. 12 P., 3 Bl., 3 P., 5 Bl., 3 P., 3 Bl., 12 P. **82nd row.**—Same as 76th row. **83rd row.**—L. 60 P., kn. 11 P., 3 Bl., 4 P., 3 Bl., 4 P., 3 Bl., 11 P., dec. 1. **84th row.**—L. 60 P., kn. 39 P. **85th row.**—L. 60 P., kn. 12 P., 2 Bl., 5 P., 1 Bl., 5 P., 2 Bl., 12 P. **86th row.**—Same as 84th row. **87th row.**—L. 60 P., kn. 12 P., 3 P., 5 Bl., 3 P., 2 Bl., 12 P. **88th row.**—Same as 84th row. **89th row.**—L. 60 P., kn. 12 P., 2 Bl., 2 P., 3 Bl., 1 P., 3 Bl., 2 P., 2 Bl., 12 P. **90th row.**—

Same as 84th row. **91st row.**—L. 60 P., dec. 1, kn. 11 P., 2 Bl., 1 P., 3 Bl., 1 P., 2 Bl., 11 P., dec. 1. **92nd row.**—L. 60 P., kn. 37 P. **93rd row.**—L. 58 P., kn. 11 P., 2 Bl., 1 P., 3 Bl., 3 P., 3 Bl., 1 P., 2 Bl., 11 P. **94th row.**—L. 58 P., kn. 37 P. **95th row.**—L. 54 P., kn. 11 P., 2 Bl., 3 P., 5 Bl., 3 P., 2 Bl., 11 P. **96th row.**—L. 54 P., kn. 37 P. **97th row.**—L. 50 P., kn. 12 P., 2 Bl., 3 P., 3 Bl., 3 P., 2 Bl., 12 P. **98th row.**—L. 50 P., kn. 37 P. **99th row.**—L. 46 P., dec. 1, kn. 11 P., 2 Bl., 4 P., 1 Bl., 4 P., 2 Bl., 11 P., dec. 1. **100th row.**—L. 46 P., kn. 35 P. **101st row.**—L. 42 P., kn. 8 P., 2 Bl., 2 P., 2 Bl., 3 P., 1 Bl., 3 P., 2 Bl., 2 P., 2 Bl., 8 P. **102nd row.**—L. 42 P., kn. 35 P. **103rd row.**—L. 38 P., kn. 7 P., 4 Bl., 1 P., 2 Bl., 3 P., 1 Bl., 3 P., 2 Bl., 1 P., 4 Bl., 7 P. **104th row.**—L. 38 P., kn. 35 P. **105th row.**—L. 34 P., kn. 7 P., 5 Bl., 1 P., 2 Bl., 5 P., 2 Bl., 1 P., 5 Bl., 7 P. **106th row.**—L. 34 P., kn. 35 P. **107th row.**—L. 30 P., dec. 1, kn. 6 P., 3 Bl., 3 P., 2 Bl., 5 P., 2 Bl., 3 P., 3 Bl., 6 P., dec. 1. **108th row.**—L. 30 P., kn. 33 P. **109th row.**—L. 26 P., kn. 6 P., 3 Bl., 3 P., 2 Bl., 5 P., 2 Bl., 3 P., 3 Bl., 6 P. **110th row.**—L. 26 P., kn. 33 P. **111th row.**—L. 22 P., kn. 7 P., 2 Bl., 3 P., 2 Bl., 5 P., 2 Bl., 3 P., 2 Bl., 7 P. **112th row.**—L. 22 P., kn. 33 P. **113th row.**—L. 18 P., kn. 7 P., 2 Bl., 3 P., 2 Bl., 5 P., 2 Bl., 3 P., 2 Bl., 7 P. **114th row.**—L. 18 P., kn. 33 P. **115th row.**—L. 14 P., dec. 1, kn. 7 P., 2 Bl., 2 P., 2 Bl., 5 P., 2 Bl., 2 P., 2 Bl., 7 P., dec. 1. **116th row.**—L. 14 P., kn. 31 P. **117th row.**—L. 10 P., kn. 8 P., 2 Bl., 1 P., 2 Bl., 5 P., 2 Bl., 1 P., 2 Bl., 8 P. **118th row.**—L. 10 P., kn. 31 P. **119th row.**—Kn. 9 P., 1 Bl., 1 P., 3 Bl., 3 P., 3 Bl., 1 P., 1 Bl., 9 P. **120th row.**—Kn. 31 P. **121st row.**—10 P., 2 Bl., 7 P., 2 Bl., 10 P. **122nd row.**—31 P. **123rd row.**—Dec. 1, 10 P., 2 Bl. 5 P., 2 Bl., 10 P., dec. 1. **124th row.**—29 P. **125th row.**—10 P., 2 Bl., 5 P., 2 Bl., 10 P. **126th row.**—29 P. **127th row.**—Same as 125th row. **128th row.**—29 P. **129th row.**—6 P., 2 Bl., 2 P., 2 Bl., 5 P., 2 Bl., 2 P., 2 Bl., 6 P. **130th row.**—29 P. **131st row.**—Dec. 1, 4 P., 4 Bl. 2 P., 2 Bl., 3 P., 2 Bl., 2 P., 4 Bl., 4 P., dec. 1. **132nd row.**—27 P. **133rd row.**—4 P., 5 Bl., 1 P., 2 Bl., 3 P., 2 Bl., 1 P., 5 Bl., 4 P. **134th row.**—27 P. **135th row.**—4 P., 3 Bl., 3 P., 2 Bl., 3 P., 2 Bl., 3 P., 3 Bl., 4 P. **136th row.**—27 P. **137th row.**—4 P., 2 Bl., 4 P., 2 Bl., 3 P., 2 Bl., 4 P., 2 Bl., 4 P. **138th row.**—27 P. **139th row.**—Dec. 1, 3 P., 2 Bl., 4 P., 2 Bl., 3 P., 2 Bl., 4 P., 2 Bl., 3 P., dec. 1. **140th row.**—25 P. **141st row.**—4 P., 2 Bl., 3 P., 2 Bl., 3 P., 2 Bl., 3 P., 2 Bl., 4 P. **142nd row.**—25 P. **143rd row.**—5 P., 2 Bl., 2 P., 2 Bl., 3 P., 2 Bl., 2 P., 2 Bl., 5 P. **144th row.**—25 P. **145th row.**—6 P., 1 Bl., 2 P., 2 Bl., 3 P., 2

Concluded on page 15

No. 620

The HOMESTEAD No. 620
Smart Crocheted Bag in Navy and Steel, Pyramid upon Pyramid.
Made with HEMINWAY SILKS

Materials: No. 666 Navy, 3 spools Purse Twist, 9 bunches Steel Beads Nos. 8 or 9, 1 Steel Crochet Needle, No. 11.

Bottom of Bag: String 2 bunches beads (B.) on silk, ch. 5, join.

1st row.—7 s. c. in ring. (Size of finished bag 8 inches long, 6½ inches wide at center.) **2nd row.**—2 s. c. in each s. c. (14 s. c. in row). **3rd row.**—* 1 s. c. in s. c., 1 s. c. with B. in next s. c., 1 s. c. without B. in same st., * repeat, having 7 sections. **4th row.**—* 1 s. c. in s. c., 2 s. c. with B. in next 2 sts., 1 s. c. without B. in same st. for inc., * repeat around. Continue inc. in same manner until you have 10 B. in each section. **13th row.**—* 1 s. c. in s. c., 11 s. c. with B., 1 s. c. in same st., Push 3 inches beads B. toward needle (1½ inches L.), * repeat around. Continue inc. 1 B. in each section until there are 17 B. to a section. **20th row.**—18 B. in each section with a L. Stringing 2½ inches of B. (1¼ inches) as directed in 13th row. Continue inc. until you have 24 B. in each section. **26th row.**—1 L. stringing 2 inches of B. (1 inch) between each beaded section as in the 13th row. **27th row.**—1 s. c., 1 s. c. over B., 23 B., 1 s. c. over last B., repeat around. Continue dec. B. until there is 1 B. in each section, * 1 s. c. over B., 25 B. over s. c., * repeat around. Dec. 1 B. on both sides until there is 1 B. in each section.

Tr. C. Band: Ch. 4 for 1 tr. c., 1 tr. c. (silk over needle twice) in next st., * push 5 B. toward needle, insert needle in next or 3rd st. of previous row, pull L. through, silk over, pull through both L., pull up a long L. to cover B., silk over, pull through L., silk over, pull through 2 remaining L., 2 tr. c., * repeat from * to * around, join. Repeat this row 2 more times having the L. on the 1st tr. c. of previous row, 1 row s. c. in each st. of previous row, then on next row, dec. 1 st. every 10th st. until you have 168 sts. around bag, 1 more row s. c.

2nd Pyramid Band: 1 s. c., 23 B., repeat around, dec. 1 B. on both sides of sections until there is 1 B. in each section with 23 s. c. between.

2nd Tr. C. Band: Same as 1st band, 1 row s. c., then dec. 1 st. every 13th st. until there are 154 sts. in row, 1 more row s. c.

3rd Pyramid Band: * 1 s. c., 21 B., * repeat around, dec. 1 B. on both sides of sections until there is 1 B. in each section with 21 s. c. between, 4 rows s. c.

Loops: ** s. c. with B. over 19 s. c., * turn, ch. 1, s. c. over 6 sts. without B., turn, ch. 1, 1 s. c. in 1st st., 4 s. c. with B. in next 4 sts., 1 s. c. without B. in last st., * continue from * to * until there are 6 B. rows, turn, work back and forth for 12 s. c. rows without B., attach to starting point of L., ch. 4, fasten other end of L., ** repeat from ** to ** for 8 L. in row.

Cords: With 3 threads of silk, ch. 4, 1 d. c. in 1st ch., turn, ch. 4, 1 d. c. in next st., repeat for 22 inches. Make another cord of same length and draw through beading from opposite sides, join neatly.

SOU LE BRAS PAISLEY BAG No. 598
Concluded from page 13

Concluded from page 13

Bl., 2 P., 1 Bl., 6 P. **146th row.**—25 P. **147th row.**—Dec. 1, 6 P., 1 Bl., 1 P., 2 Bl., 3 P., 2 Bl., 1 P., 1 Bl., 6 P., dec. 1. **148th row.**—23 P. **149th row.**—6 P., 4 Bl., 3 P., 4 Bl., 6 P. **150th row.**—23 P. **151st row.**—7 P., 2 Bl., 5 P., 2 Bl., 7 P. **152nd row.**—23 P. **153rd row.**—Same as 151st row. **154th row.**—23 P. **155th row.**—Dec. 1, 7 P., 2 Bl., 3 P., 2 Bl., 7 P., dec. 1. **156th row.**—21 P. **157th row.**—7 P., 2 Bl., 3 P., 2 Bl., 7 P. **158th row.**—21 P. **159th row.**—Same as 157th row. **160th row.**—21 P. **161st row.**—8 P., 2 Bl., 1 P., 2 Bl., 8 P. **162nd row.**—21 P. **163rd row.**—Dec. 1, 7 P., 2 Bl., 1 P., 2 Bl., 7 P., dec. 1. **164th row.**—19 P. **165th row.**—7 P., 2 Bl., 1 P., 2 Bl., 7 P. **166th row.**—19 P. **167th row.**—Same as 165th row. **168th row.**—19 P. **169th row.**—4 P., 2 Bl., 1 P., 2 Bl., 1 P., 2 Bl., 1 P., 2 Bl., 4 P. **170th row.**—19 P. **171st row.**—Dec. 1, 2 P., 1 Bl., 3 P., 2 Bl., 1 P., 2 Bl., 3 P., 1 Bl., 2 P., dec. 1. **172nd row.**—17 P. **173rd row.**—2 P., 1 Bl., 3 P., 2 Bl., 1 P., 2 Bl., 3 P., 1 Bl., 2 P. **174th row.**—17 P. **175th row.**—2 P., 6 Bl., 1 P., 6 Bl., 2 P. **176th row.**—17 P. **177th row.**—3 P., 4 Bl., 3 P., 4 Bl., 3 P. **178th row.**—17 P. **179th to 183rd rows.**—17 P. **183rd row.**—7 P., 3 Bl., 7 P. **184th row.**—17 P. **185th row.**—5 P., 7 Bl., 5 P. **186th row.**—17 P. **187th row.**—3 P., 11 Bl., 3 P. **188th row.**—17 P. **189th row.**—1 P., 15 Bl., 1 P. **190th row.**—17 P. **191st row.**—17 B. **192nd row.**—17 P. **193rd row.**—7 Bl., 3 P., 7 Bl. **194th row**—17 P. **195th row.**—5 Bl., 7 P., 5 Bl. **196th row.**—17 P. **197th row.**—3 Bl., 11 P., 3 Bl. **198th row.**—17 P. **199th row.**—1 Bl., 15 P., 1 Bl. **200th to 221st rows.**—17 P. This is just half of the bag. Repeat 219th to 1st row and bind off. Sew around bottom. Join L. at side with crochet needle, slip st. a L. from each side together, 3 chains with Bl. B. on each ch., slip st. next 2 L. and so on up side, do other side same way.

To Line: Lay bag flat on table and cut an exact pattern of same, double lining and cut pattern, French seam the body together making the seam wide enough to insert a ribbon wire to hold out the beaded loops, left free when knitting. Tack these in position as shown in illustration and sl. st. the silk to handle throughout its entire length. It is very simple to put together and most unusual in treatment. It may be closed by snap button or ring if desired.

The WILDFLOWER No. 619
A Smart Evening Bag Knitted in White with Pastel Beads.
Illustrated on page 24
Made with HEMINWAY SILKS

Illustrated on page 24

Materials: Nos. 3 or 4 White or Cream, 2 spools Purse Twist; 20 bunches Pastel Glass Beads; ¼ yd. Silk to Line Bag; 1 Pair Steel Knitting Needles, No. 16; 1 Steel Crochet Needle, No. 8 or 9.

Top of Bag: String 2 bunches of Beads (B.) on 1 spool of silk (when necessary to string more B. join twist always at end of a row), cast on 48 sts. Knit (kn.) 3 plain, * insert needle in next st., slip 1 B., complete st., kn. 3, repeat from * ending with kn. 3 plain. Kn. 5 rows sl. 1 B., kn. 5 rows sl. 2 B., kn. 5 rows sl. 3 B., kn. 5 rows sl. 4 B., kn. 10 rows sl. 5 B., kn. 12 rows sl. 6 B., kn. 12 rows sl. 7 B. This completes one-half of bag, reverse to beginning. Sew up sides of bag.

Tabs: Cast on 7 sts., kn. 2, sl. 1 B., sl. 1 B. in each of next 3 sts., kn. 1 plain, kn. back plain, continue 2 rows for 16 rows, bind off. There are 12 tabs. Sew to top of bag and run cord through.

Cords: With 2 threads, ch. 6 and join. Work round and round with s. c., picking up the outside thread only, thus having the wrong side of st. to show. Make 2 cords 20 inches long.

Lining: Cut silk shape of bag and line neatly, sl. st. to top of bag and fasten at corners.

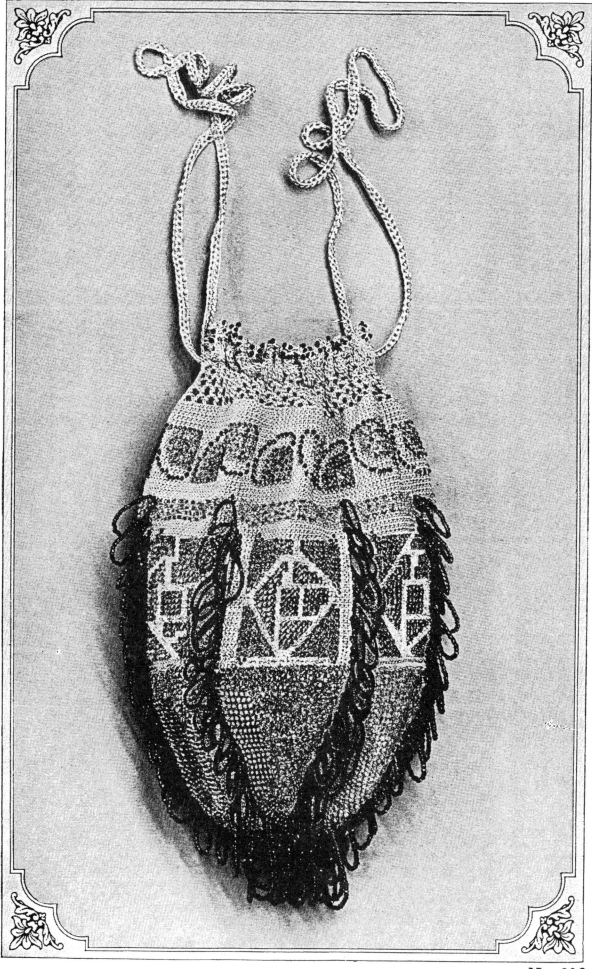

No. 606

The ROSEMOORE No. 606

Softly Blended Shades of Beads gives the "Derniere Touche" in Coloring and Effect. The Outline of Black Loops between Sections forms a Lovely Finishing Touch Bringing Out Well the Complementary Colors of Beads and Silk.

Made with **HEMINWAY SILKS**

Materials.—No. 3552 Beige, 3 spools Hampton Crochet Silk; 5 bunches each Rose and Green Glass Beads; 3 bunches Amber Glass Beads; 3 bunches Black Jet Beads; 1 bunch Dark Green Beads; ¼ yd. Rose, Green or Beige Satin or Silk for Lining; 1 Steel Crochet Needle No. 10.

Direction for one of the sections, 6 of which forms bottom of bag, 2 in Green, 2 in Rose and 2 in Amber.—"Ch. 10," 1 bead (B.) in 2nd ch. from needle (9 B. in row), ch. 3, 1 B. in 1st of "ch. 3" for 1st inc. point, another B. in opposite side of "ch. 10," 8 more B. on this same side of ch., s. c. in same st. without B., s. c. in same st. with B. for 2nd inc. point, s. c. in next st. with B. on opposite side, s. c. in same st. without B., s. c. in same st. with B. for 3rd inc. point, s. c. in each st. with B. to end of row at point also on ch. to form point at bottom, ch. 3, s. c. in 1st of ch. 3, s. c. with B. to end of row at side, continue around point, keeping work flat, there are 3 inc. points, inc. each row until size of pattern illustrated. There are 28 B. in last row. Complete 6 sections and sl. st. together at back, alternating colors, Green Rose and Amber, etc.

Attach silk on which has been previously strung 1 bunch Rose B. and work 2 rows s. c. around top of bag (pattern No. 1 begins on the 1st s. c. row), **inc. 1 st. each row** on the joining sections. **3rd, 4th and 5th rows.**—Continue as per diagram on page with rose B., break silk. Then string B. beginning at 1st row of Rose section back to 22nd row and continue the pattern No. 1. 2 more rows plain s. c., dec. 4 sts. Work on last row, break silk. String 1 bunch Green B. 4 rows s. c., * 1 s. c. with B., 1

s. c. without B. * 4 more s. c. rows without B., break silk and string B. downward from 1st through the 10th row as per diagram No. 2 and complete the 5 s. c. rows without B. at top of bag.

Mesh Rows at Top of Bag.—* ch. 4 sk. 2 s. c. 1 s. c. in the 3rd s. c. * repeat around. **2nd row.**—* ch. 4, 1 s. c. over 1st mesh (m.) of previous row * repeat around. **3rd, 4th and 5th rows.**—Same as 2nd row.

Beading at Top of Bag.—Ch. 5 for 1st d. tr. c., 2 more d. tr. c. in same m., * ch. 2, 3 d. tr. c. in next m. * repeat around, there are 58 d. tr. c. groups around bag.

Triple Picot Edge with Black B.—Ch. 1, push B. toward needle, 1 s. c. in st., 2 s. c. with B. in next 2 sts., * s. c. in next st., ch. 2, push B. close to needle, ch. 2, s. c. in same st., ch. 3, 1 B., ch. 3, s. c. in same st. for middle picot, ch. 2, push B. toward needle, ch. 2, s. c. in same st., s. c. with B. in next 3 sts. * repeat around ending with triple picot, break silk.

Cords.—2 threads of silk, make a 24 inch ch., turn, s. c. on entire length of ch. and on opposite side of ch. Make 2 of these cords.

Jet Loops Outlining Each Section.—With threaded sewing needle fasten at center of bottom of bag, string 2 inches of B. (1 inch loop, L.), and fasten in same st., s. c. 3 sts., another L., continue along section ending at top of band in Green B. (19 B. L.).

Bottom Finish in Loops.—½ inch out from center of bag, attach silk and make 2 L. (1¼ inches) at center of each section. Cut lining same shape of bag. Sew up sides and sl. st. to last row of s. c. around top of bag, fasten at very bottom.

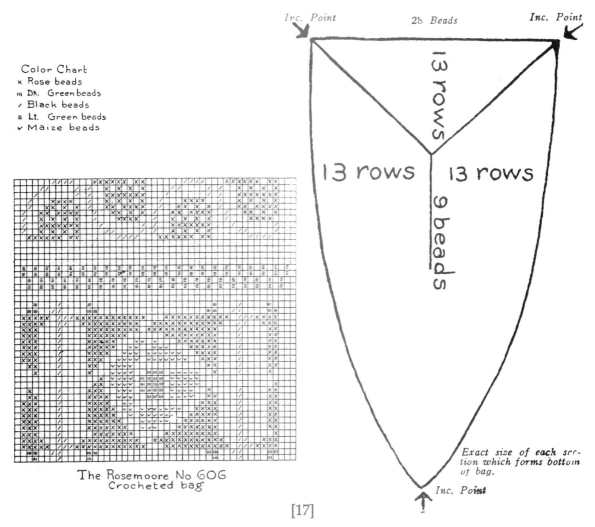

Color Chart
x Rose beads
ɯ Dk. Green beads
⁄ Black beads
≡ Lt. Green beads
ᵥ Maize beads

The Rosemoore No 606
Crocheted bag

Exact size of each section which forms bottom of bag.

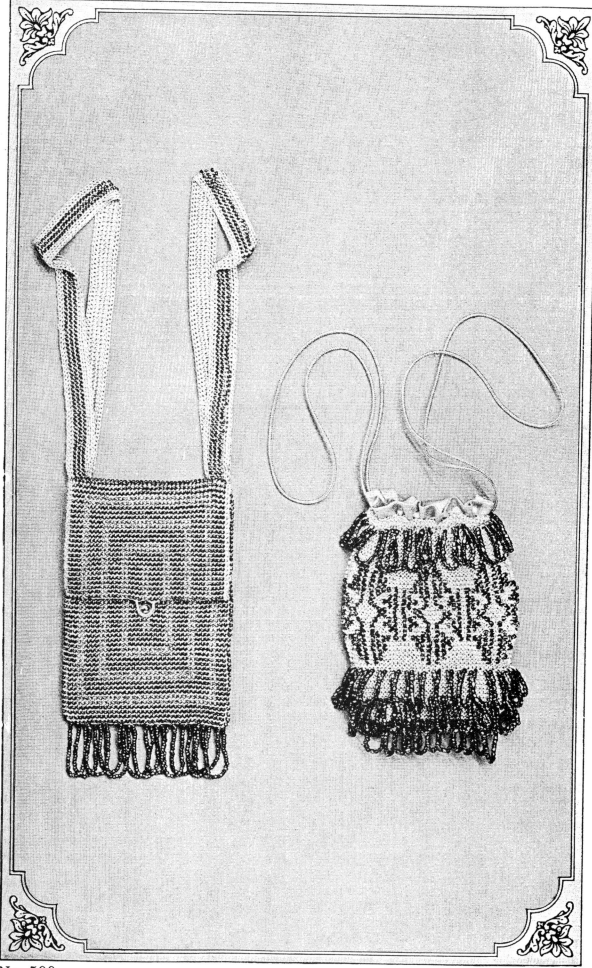

No. 599 [18] Directions for 617 on page 34 No. 617

The MARY LEE VANITIÉ BAG No. 599

Made with HEMINWAY SILKS

Materials: No. 830 Grey, 1 spool Hampton Crochet Silk; 2 bunches Henna Color Metal Beads, 1 bunch Steel Beads, Nos. 8 or 9; 1 Small Round Silver Color Button, ⅛ yd. Sheer Silk for lining; Steel Crochet Needle, No. 11.

Note: The Crocheting is commenced always from one side of bag, this necessitates the cutting of silk at end of row, leaving about 1 inch length of silk on **each side of work**—the crocheting must be done very tightly, always keeping the first and last sts. of each row firm in s. c. without bead (B.). Length of finished bag before making up 10½ inches—width, 3 inches; length, folded, 4½ inches.

Ch. 40 sts.   H.—Henna Beads.   S.—Steel Beads.

1st row.—1 s. c. without B. in each ch., 40 s. c.   **2nd row.**—1 s. c., 38 H., 1 s. c.   **3rd to 25th rows.**—Same as 2nd row.   **25th to 32nd rows.**—1 s. c., 3 H., 2 S., 3 H., 2 S., 3 H., 2 S., 3 H., 2 S., 3 H., 2 S., 3 H., 2 S., 3 H., 1 s. c.   **32nd to 35th rows.**—1 s. c., 3 H., 2 S., 3 H., 2 S., 3 H., 2 S., 8 H., 2 S., 3 H., 2 S., 3 H., 2 S., 3 H., 1 s. c.   **35th to 37th rows.**—1 s. c., 3 H., 2 S., 3 H., 2 S., 3 H., 12 S., 3 H., 2 S., 3 H., 2 S., 3 H., 1 s. c.   **37th to 40th rows.**—1 s. c., 3 H., 2 S., 3 H., 2 S., 18 H., 2 S., 3 H., 2 S., 3 H., 1 s. c.   **40th to 42nd rows.**—1 s. c., 3 H., 2 S., 3 H., 22 S., 3 H., 2 S., 3 H., 1 s. c.   **42nd to 45th rows.**—1 s. c., 3 H., 2 S., 28 H., 2 S., 3 H., 1 s. c.   **45th and 46th rows.**—1 s. c., 3 H., 32 S., 3 H., 1 s. c.   **47th to 105th rows.**—1 s. c., 38 H., 1 s. c.   **105th and 106th rows.**—1 s. c., 3 H., 32 S., 3 H., 1 s. c.   **107th to 110th rows.**—1 s. c., 3 H., 2 S., 28 H., 2 S., 3 H., 1 s. c.   **110th and 111th rows.**—1 s. c., 3 H., 2 S., 3 H., 22 S., 3 H., 2 S., 3 H., 1 s. c.   **112th to 115th rows.**—1 s. c., 3 H., 2 S., 3 H., 2 S., 18 H., 2 S., 3 H., 2 S., 3 H., 1 s. c.   **115th to 117th rows.**—1 s. c., 3 H., 2 S., 3 H., 2 S., 3 H., 12 S., 3 H., 2 S., 3 H., 2 S., 3 H., 1 s. c.   **117th to 120th rows.**—1 s. c., 3 H., 2 S., 3 H., 2 S., 3 H., 2 S., 8 H., 2 S., 3 H., 2 S., 3 H., 2 S., 3 H., 1 s. c.   **120th to 127th rows.**—1 s. c., 3 H., 2 S., 3 H., 2 S., 3 H., 2 S., 3 H., 2 S., 3 H., 2 S., 3 H., 2 S., 3 H., 1 s. c.

Handles: 1st row.—Ch. 4, s. c. in 2nd st. from needle with B., 2 more s. c. with B., ch. 1, turn.   **2nd row.**—4 s. c. on 4 s. c., without B.   **3rd row.**—Ch. 1, 4 s. c. with B. on 4 s. c. of previous row. Repeat 2nd and 3rd rows for 9 or 10 inches in length. Before sewing up sides of bag, cut lining of same shape, then sew up sides of bag, also lining, slip lining into pocket of bag and sl. st. around lap and front. Close with loop at center of lap and button in place. Sew the handle ends in side of pocket, 2 may be used as shown on illustration.

Fringe: At bottom consists of 14 (1 inch) loops in Henna.

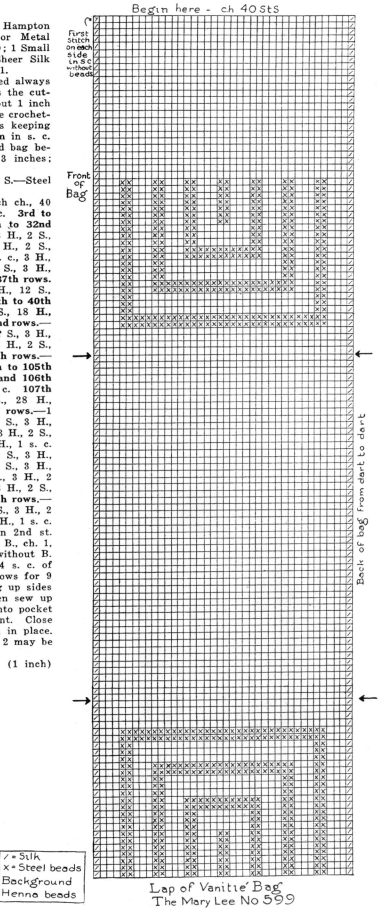

Begin here - ch 40 sts

First Stitch on each side in s c without beads

Front of Bag

Back of bag from dart to dart

/ = Silk
x = Steel beads
Background
Henna beads

Lap of Vanitié Bag
The Mary Lee No 599

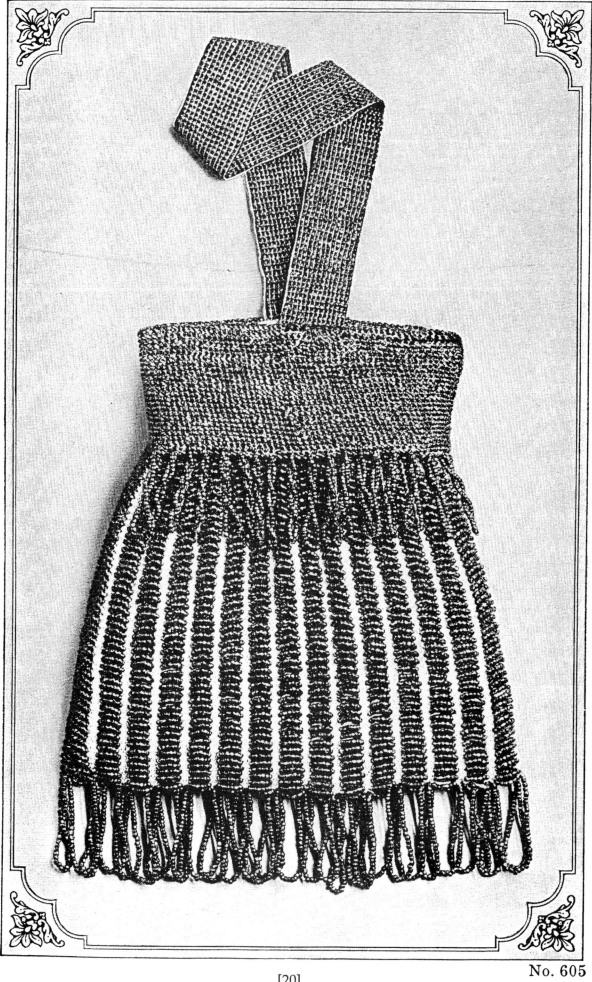

No. 605

The INWOOD POUCH No. 605

Knitted Novelty Bag—Ever Old and Always New.

Made with HEMINWAY SILKS

Materials: No. 4 Cream, 2 spools Purse Twist; 35 bunches Bronze Iridescent Beads; 1 pair Steel Knitting Needles, No. 16; 1 Steel Crochet Needle, No. 9.

Begin at Top: String 2 bunches of Beads (B.) on silk, cast on 48 sts., knit (kn.) 10 ridges (R.) (20 rows). (When necessary to string more B. join silk at end of row.) **11th row.**—Kn. 3 plain, * insert needle in next st., slip 1 B., complete st., kn. 2 plain, repeat from * across row. **12th row.**—Same as 11th R. **13th and 14th ridges.**—Loop (L.) of 2 beads. (Loops extend crosswise of Bag.) **15th, 16th and 17th ridges.**—L. of 3 B. **18th, 19th and 20th ridges.**—L. of 4 B. **21st, 22nd and 23rd ridges.**—L. of 5 B. **24th through 65th ridges.**—L. of 6 B. (½ of bag—width at bottom, 7½ inches x 6½ inches in length.) Continue in reverse order. Sew up sides of bag.

Fringe: Thread sewing needle with Purse Twist, fasten in bottom corner, string 50 beads, fasten thread, string 50 beads, fasten thread to last B. of 1st beaded L., * string 50 B., fasten to 1st B. of next beaded L., string 50 B., fasten to last B. of same beaded L., * repeat across bottom of bag having 31 L.

Cuff: String 2 bunches of B., ch. 120 (10½ inches), join in ring, s. c. in each ch. with B. as follows: insert needle in ch., push B. close to needle, silk over needle, pull L. through, silk over, pull through both L. on needle, continue around for 25 B. rows more (2 in. wide), on the L. or 27th row, * 2 s. c. with B. in 1st 2 sts., 1 (1½ inch L.) or about 50 B. in next st., * continue around, break silk and sew to top of knitted section.

Wrist Strap: Using Bead Loom, 15 silk threads of warp, 14 beads in each row, about 1 inch wide. Strap should be 14 inches long, and can be either knitted or crocheted.

To Line Around Top of Bag: Sew a piece of ribbon wire to give shape to bag, also sew to inside of cuff if desired, 2 pieces of this same wire, cut satin or taffeta lining same shape as bag, sl. st. neatly to last beaded row after the joining of beaded handle.

FROM FLORENY No. 611

Illustrated on page 36

Small Knitted Evening Bag.

Made with HEMINWAY SILKS

Materials: No. 653 Shrimp Pink, 4 spools Concord Crochet Silk; 2 bunches Opal or Satin Beads (1,200 to a bunch); 1 pair No. 2 Short Bone Knitting Needles, 1 Steel Crochet Needle, No. 9.

With silk, cast on 52 sts.

1st row.—Knit (kn.) 1 row plain. **2nd row.**—Kn. row placing 1 bead (B.) in each st. as follows: (push B. toward needle, silk over, kn. the st.), continue across with 1 B. in each st. (8 inches across). Continue for 32 more B. rows always having a plain kn. row between (34 rows in all, 5 inches in depth). Bind off and sew the bottom and sides together.

Loops of Beads Around Bag: Thread fine sewing needle with silk and count 24 B. or measure 2 inches for each loop (L.), fasten well and run needle about ¾ inch down seam, attach another 2 inch L., continue placing 7 L. along each side, 1 L. directly on each corner at bottom with 6 L. in between.

Beading: Attach Pink silk and with No. 9 crochet needle, 1 s. c. in each st. around top of bag. **2nd row.**—Ch. 5 for 1st d. tr. c. (silk over needle 3 times, * silk over, pull through 2 sts., * repeat 2 times more), 2 more d. tr. c. in next 2 sts., * ch. 3, 3 d. tr. c. in next 3 sts., *, 18 d. tr. c. groups around bag, close and turn. **3rd row.**—* 5 s. c. in the 1st 5 sts., 1 picot (P.) in same 5th st., thus: ch. 3, s. c. in st., ch. 5, s. c. in same st., ch. 3, s. c. in same 5th st., * repeat around.

Cords: Using 3 threads, ch. 1 loosely, * silk over needle, insert needle in ch. 1, silk over, pull L. through ch., silk over, pull through all L. on needle, * repeat * to * for 20 inches, make a 2nd cord of same length and draw through beading from opposite sides of bag and fasten neatly.

The BRAE BURN No. 601

Concluded from page 9

rows same as 3rd row, inc. on each of the 4 corners always on s. c. without B. (124 s. c. in last row), 2 more rows of s. c. without B., inc. in same manner on inc. points (140 s. c. in last row). Bottom about 3 inches square, break silk. **18th row.**—String 3 bunches of B. on Henna No. 2032, working from diagram on 1st row of design (the check represents beads), * 3 s. c. B., 27 s. c. silk only (S.), 3 s. c. B., 2 s. c. S., 3 s. c. B., 27 s. c. S., 3 s. c. B., 2 s. c. S. * repeat from * to * once more around bag (which has 4 sides). **19th and 20th rows.**—Same as 18th row. Continue as per diagram which is ½ of bag only, repeat pattern again throughout each row for 2nd half of bag breaking silk and attaching new shades as noted in 39th, 55th, 69th, 81st to 92nd or last row.

2 Strings: Using No. 4 Crochet Needle and 5 threads of silk (Henna, Tangerine and the remainder of silk left), ch. 1 loosely, silk over needle, insert needle in ch. 1, * silk over, pull loop (L.) through, silk over, pull L. through all L. on needle, silk over, insert needle in L. *, continue for 24 inches for each string.

Cord Ornaments: Using 5 threads of Tangerine for each strand, braid 4 inches and wind twice around a pencil to form a ball shape. draw cords through, placing one directly on edge of bag and another 1½ inches above (8 are needed). a fancy ring slips over the cords to close the bag.

Fringe at Bottom: Thread sewing needle and fasten silk at one corner of bag on plain rows in Brown, thread on silk 2⅜ inches of beads, turn, run needle through 5 B. from end, back through the string of B. and run silk in bag, sk. 1 s. c., run silk in next st., repeat 4 times on each side of B. strand at corner (9 bead fringes around each corner), continue around.

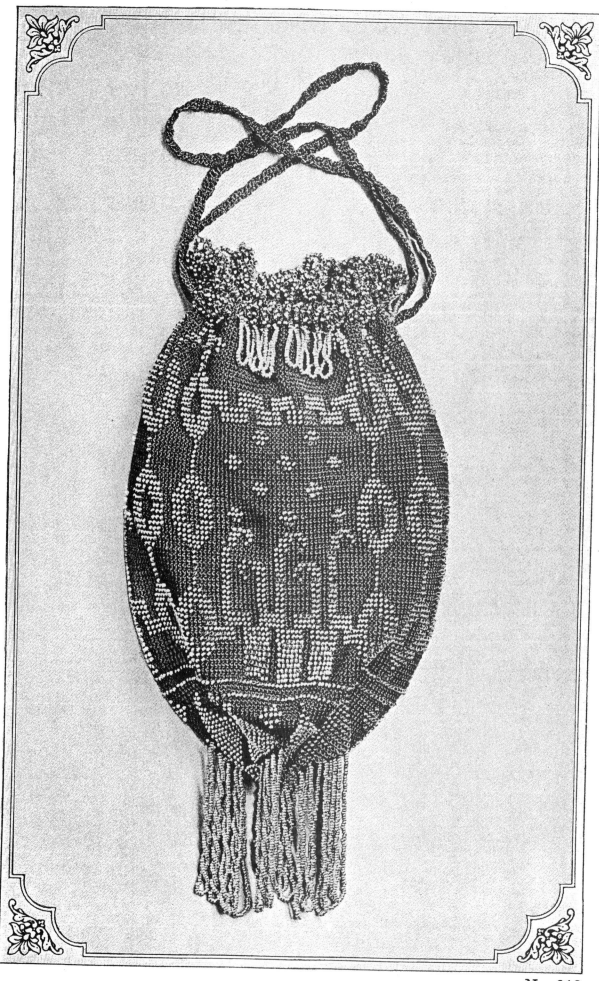

No. 612

The CONTINENTAL No. 612

Round Empire Bag with Design Crocheted in Steel Beads.

Made with HEMINWAY SILKS

Materials: No. 2285 Tangerine or No. 666 Navy, 3 spools Hampton Crochet Silk; 9 bunches No. 8 round (uncut) Steel Beads; 1 Steel Crochet Needle, No. 10.

Bottom of Bag: String 2 bunches of beads (B.) on spool of silk, ch. 3, join in ring. **1st row.**—6 s. c. in ring. **2nd row.**—2 s. c. with B. in each st., continue around. **3rd row.**—* 2 s. c. with B. in 1st st., 1 s. c. with B. in next st., * repeat * to * around always (18 sts.). **4th row.**—* 2 s. c. with B. in 1st st., 1 s. c. with B. in each of next 2 sts., * (24 sts.). **5th row.**—* 2 s. c. with B. in 1st st., 1 s. c. with B. in each of next 3 sts., * (32 sts.). **6th row.**—* 1 s. c. with B., 3 s. c. without B., * repeat 7 times more to form 8 sections. Inc. 1 B. in every section until there are 10 B. in each, also inc. in the 3rd st. between sections. Continue inc. in same st. every row and dec. 1 B. until you have 5 B. with 10 sts. between. **Next row.**—* 4 s. c. with B., 5 s. c., 1 s. c. with B., 5 s. c., inc. on last or same st. of each section, * in this and following rows. **Next row.**—* 3 B., 5 s. c., 3 B., 5 s. c., inc. in last or same st. *. **Next row.**—* 2 B., 5 s. c., 5 B., 5 s. c., inc. in last st. *. **Next row.**—* 2 B., 7 s. c., 3 B., 7 s. c., inc. in last st. *. **Next row.**—* 1 B., 9 s. c., 1 B., 9 s. c., inc. in last st., * 1 row s. c. without B. 1 row s. c. with B. if there are not 167 sts. in this row inc. in next rows at intervals until that number is reached. 3 rows s. c. without B. Begin pattern following diagram to top of bag, the checked spaces represent beads,

open spaces s. c. in silk without B. Finish at top with 1 row s. c. without B.

Beading: Ch. 5 for 1st d. tr. c. (silk around needle 3 times, insert needle in st., silk over needle, pull loop (L.) through st., * push B. close to needle, silk over, pull through 2 sts., * repeat 3 times more, this is 2nd d. tr. c.), 1 more d. tr. c. with B., silk over needle 3 times, insert needle in st., silk over, pull L. through, measure 1¾ inch of B. and push toward needle to form B. L., * silk over, pull through 2 sts., * repeat * to * 3 times more, this makes 4 d. tr. c. without B., repeat around (there is always 1 L. on the plain d. tr. c.). 1 row s. c. with B. in each st. of previous row.

Mesh Row: * 7 ch. with B. in each ch. st., sk. 3 s. c., s. c. in next st., * repeat around. **2nd row.**—Sl. st. into each st. to center of m., * ch. 6, with B. in each ch., s. c. in center of next m. *. **3rd row.**—Sl. st. into each st. to center of m., ch. 5, s. c. in center of next m. **4th row.**—Same as 3rd row, break silk.

Cords: Ch. 5, d. c. in 2nd ch., d. c. in 1st ch., ch. 3, * 2 d. c. on d. c., ch. 3, turn, * continue or 20 inches. Make a 2nd cord and run through beading.

Fringe at Bottom of Bag: 5 loops of 2½ inches in 1st section, 4 L. in 3rd section, 5 L. in 5th section, 4 L. in 7th section. Cut lining shape of bag, sew up sides and sl. st. to top of bag, fasten at bottom.

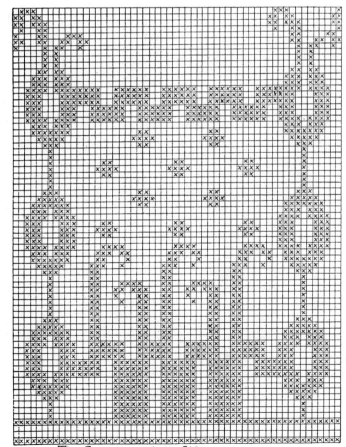

Repeat section shown twice more There are three patterns worked in steel beads around bag

The Continentale' No 612
Crocheted Bag

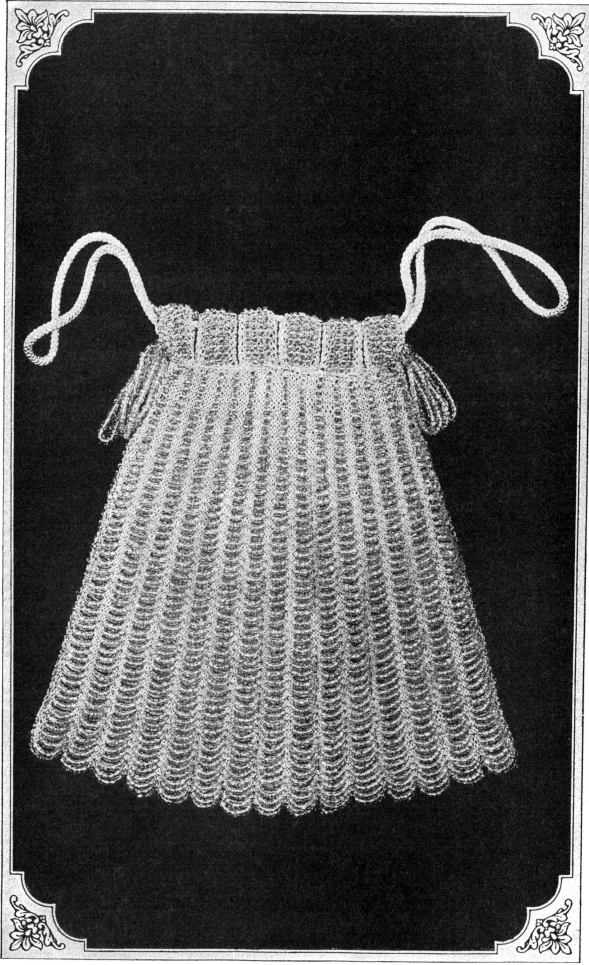

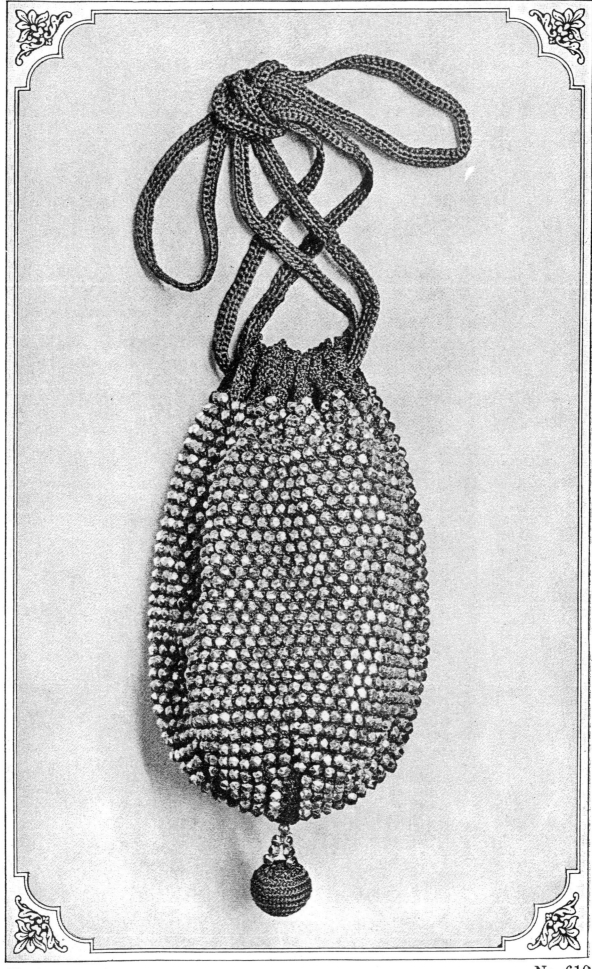

The INDO-CHINESE No. 602

Especially Smart Knitted Bag, an Attractive Accessory to the Finest Frock or Tailleur.

Made with *HEMINWAY SILKS*

Materials: No. 3512 Tan, 2 spools Purse Twist; 10 bunches Navy Blue Beads, 10 bunches Crystal Beads, 3 bunches Red or Rose Beads, 2 bunches Peach or Green Beads; ½ yd. White or Black Ribbon Wire; 5 Knitting Needles, No. 18. *Concluded on page 29*

×	Navy Blue beads
ɪɪɪ	Pink or Red beads
≡	Peach or Green beads
	Background
	White crystal beads

71 Stitches across — 93 Rows in length

Indo-Chinese Bag No. 602

No. 613

The WAINWRIGHT No. 613

Round Knitted Bag—Ample in Size and Pleasing to a Quiet, Refined Taste.

Made with HEMINWAY SILKS

Materials: No. 2290 Jade, 1 spool Purse Twist; No. 85 Dark Green, 1 spool Purse Twist; 12 bunches Green Iridescent Beads, 8 bunches Amber Glass Beads; 2 (1¼ inch) Button Molds, 4 small round Molds; 4 Steel Knitting Needles, No. 18; 1 Steel Crochet Needle, No. 10.

String 2 bunches Green Iridescent Beads (B.) on spool of Jade.

Bottom of Bag: Cast on 8 sts. on 3 needles (3, 3 and 2 sts. respectively). Knit (kn.) off 1st row. (Size of finished bag, 6¼ inches wide at center x 8½ inches long.) **2nd row.**—Inc. 1 every other st. by kn. off 1 st. on back loop of st. and 1 on front (after this row all kn. is done on back st., pushing B. through st. before kn. off so as to have it on front or right side of bag, this is easily done; a little patience is required in working out the 1st few rows). **3rd row.**—Kn. off 2 sts. with B., inc. on 2nd B. 1 st. **without B.**, kn. around bag thus dividing in 6 sections for inc. points. Inc. every row in same manner until you have 140 sts. on needle. Kn. around plain for 3 rows, this brings you to border, break silk.

Note: Checked squares represent Amber Beads, and open squares are Green Beads.

Grecian Border: Unwind a few yards of Jade silk and string Green and Amber B. (with B. needle) row by row, beginning at top of border and string-ing downwards. Attach silk and kn. upwards to end of border, break silk. String B. for 4 rows of plain Green Iridescent, this brings you to center design which runs in diagonal bands (a timely suggestion in the threading of B. is to string B. downwards for 1 of the 3 sections at a time) there are 7 diagonal bands in Amber B. with 11 sts. of Green B. always between. Kn. upwards according to diagram, this completes design. Break silk and string for border lines, 4 rows Green, 1 row Amber, 1 row Green, 2 rows Amber, 15 rows Green, bind off.

Loop Finish at Top of Bag: Using crochet needle and Dark Green silk with Green B., working from underside of bag, * s. c. across 14 sts. with B. in each st., turn (1 s. c. in each s. c. of last 4 sts., turn 4 s. c. with B. in 4 s. c. of previous row), continue turning and working until you have 7 rows with B. 4 more rows without B. Attach to corner at beginning of L., ch. 5, attach ch. to opposite corner of L. and bag, * repeat from * to * 9 times more, there are 10 L. around top of bag.

Cords for Top of Bag: In Green silk, using 2 threads, ch. 24 inches, turn, s. c. on 2nd st. from needle, s. c. in each ch. to end of row, turn, s. c. on opposite side of ch. to end, break silk. 2 cords are needed, run cords through L. from opposite sides of bag and join neatly.

Buttons: String on Green silk the Amber B., ch. 3, join, 6 s. c. in ring. **2nd row.**—* s. c. with B. in 1st s. c., 2 s. c. with B. in next st., * repeat (9 sts.). **3rd row.**—* s. c. in 1st 2 sts., 2 s. c. in next st. *. **4th row.**—* s. c. in 4 sts., 2 s. c. in next st. *. **5th row.**—* s. c. in 5 sts., 2 s. c. in next st. *. **6th row.**—* s. c. in 6 sts., 2 s. c. in next st. *. **7th row.**—* s. c. in 7 sts., 2 s. c. in next st. *. **8th row.**—* s. c. in 8 sts., 2 s. c. in next st. *. **9th row.**—* s. c. in 9 sts., 2 s. c. in next st., *. Insert mold, s. c. round and round, dec. to close, make another in same manner. 4 small round molds are needed, string Green B. on Green silk, ch. 3, join in ring. 4 s. c. with B. in ring.

2nd, 3rd and 4th rows.—Inc. 4 sts. in every row, insert mold and s. c. with B., dec. to close, leave ¼ yd. of silk to thread in sewing needle, string 2 inches of Amber B. and fasten in loop, cover another mold in same manner. Cover the 3rd and 4th molds and place 2 loops on each. Sew large molds in position on each side of very bottom of bag and fasten ball pendants between molds as shown in illustration. Balls with 2 loops are placed on sides fastening 1 loop on each side of bag. Cut lining same shape of bag, sew up sides, and sl. st. around top of bag. Fasten at bottom.

15 more rows green iridescent beads to top of bag

Open mesh in green beads   The Wainwright No. 613   Design in amber beads
Knitted bag

The INDO-CHINESE No. 602

Concluded from page 27

String 2 bunches Navy Blue Beads (B.) on silk, cast on 142 sts., divide on 4 needles (35, 35, 36, 36 sts. respectively), join. **1st row.**—Knit (kn.) 1 row plain (pl.). **2nd row.**—Kn. around with 1 B. in each st. as follows: (needle in back of st., push B. toward needle, pull B. through st. along with silk), continue around. (Size of bag, 6½ x 8 inches.) **3rd to 7th row.**—Same as 2nd row, break silk. String B. according to colorings as noted by characters indicated on diagram, which is one side of bag, repeat each row once more for opposite side of bag, stringing about 10 rows at a time, starting from 17th row of design, stringing to 7th row. Continue knitting following diagram. Work on 142 sts. to the 82nd row, then dec. 1 st. on each side of bag (to dec.: kn. 2 sts. together), continue dec. and following diagram until there are 94 sts. left, bind off. Sew up bottom.

To Line: Line bag with Rose or any color satin desired after the ribbon wire has been sewed around ½ inch below top of bag to give the bag body and shape.

Casing for Draw Strings: Run a line of stitching ½ inch from top, following with a 2nd line ¾ inch below the first.

Strings: Ch. 24 inches (not too tightly), 1 d. c. in 5th ch. from needle, 1 d. c. in each ch. across, turn. **2nd row.**—Ch. 3, 1 d. c. in each d. c. of previous row, fasten and break silk. Complete a 2nd string and draw through casing, from opposite sides of bag.

Fringe: Beginning at 1st row of dec., attach silk, with Blue B., measure 4 inches (2 inch Loop), attach to within ½ inch from starting point, continue in this manner across bottom of bag until you reach the same point on opposite side. Sew 1 more row of 2 inch loops between the loops of previous row.

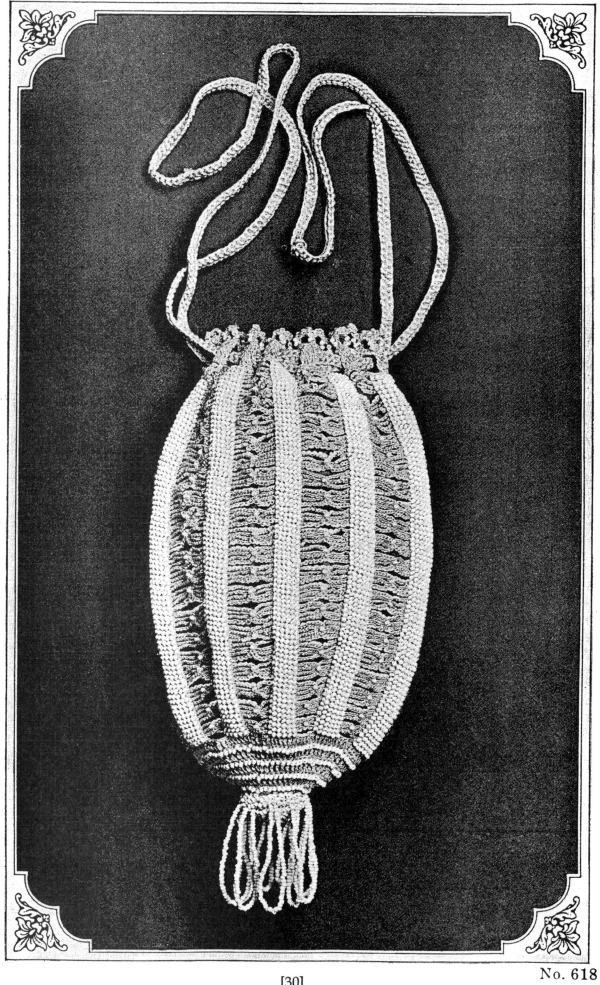

No. 618

The RICHELIEU No. 618

A Charming Little Lacey Bag that
Adds Quaintness to the Period Frock.

Made with HEMINWAY SILKS

Materials: Nos. 3 White, 2 spools Purse Twist; 7 long Bunches White Chalk Beads; 1 Button Mold (1¼ inches diameter); 1 Steel Crochet Needle, No. 11.

Bottom of Bag: String 1 bunch of beads (B.) on 1 spool of silk, ch. 6, join in ring (R.). **1st row.**—9 s. c. in R. **2nd row.**—Tr. c. in each s. c., always ch. 1 between each tr. c. (9 tr. c.). **3rd row.**—1 tr. c. in each tr. c. and ch. of previous row, 18 tr. c. **4th row.**—1 tr. c. on tr. c. and ch.; 36 tr. c. in row. **5th or 1st bead row.**—S. c. with B. in each tr. c. and ch., inc. at intervals so there are 48 B. at end of row. **Inc. is always done on the ch. 6th row.**—Tr. c. in each s. c. and ch. 1, 48 tr. c. **7th row.**—S. c. with B. on tr. c. and ch., having 69 B. in row. **8th row.**—Tr. c. in each s. c. with ch. between. **9th row.**—S. c. with B., inc. as before at intervals, 84 B. **10th row.**—Tr. c. in each s. c. with ch. 1 between. **11th row.**—S. c. with B., 110 B. **12th row.**—Ch. 1, 6 s. c. with B. on s. c., * ch. 10, sk. 5 s. c. of previous row, 6 s. c. with B. on next 6 s. c., * repeat, join. (Length of beaded bands 6¼ inches, this brings you to beading.) **13th and 14th rows.**—Same as 12th row. **15th row.**—* ch. 5, needle through **center ch.** of last 3 rows, pull loop (L.) through, push B. toward needle, silk over, pull through both L. on needle, ch. 5, 6 s. c. with B. on next 6 s. c. of previous row, * repeat.

Note: There are 10 solid B. bands around bag and B. must always lie directly over each other in same direction, each group consists of 4 ch. rows.

16th row.—Beginning of **2nd group of ch.,** ch. 11, 6 s. c. with B. on B. of previous row. **17th and 18th rows.**—Same as 16th row. **19th row.**—* ch. 6, needle through **center ch.** of last 3 rows, pull L. through, push B. toward needle, silk over, pull through both L. on needle, ch. 6, 6 s. c. with B. on next 6 sts. *. There are 6 more groups inc. 1 st. in beginning ch. row of every group until you have 18 ch. in 8th group (width 6 inches). This is center of bag. There are 11 more groups of ch. 18. This completes the 92nd row, 1 more row plain s. c.

Beading: Ch. 4 for 1st tr. c., 3 more tr. c. in next 3 sts., * ch. 4, sk. 4, 4 tr. c. in next 4 sts., * repeat.

Mesh Row.—* 4 s. c., ch. 4 for picot, sl. st. in same st., * repeat, * ch. 4, s. c., push 2 B. toward needle, insert needle in picot, pull L. through, silk over, pull through 2 L. *.

Last Row: 3 s. c. on ch., ch. 4 for picot, s. c. in same st. to close.

Cords: Using 3 threads, ch. 24 inches, 1 s. c. in 2nd ch. from needle, s. c. in each ch. to end, break silk. Make a 2nd cord, draw through beading from opposite sides of bag and fasten neatly.

Mold: Cover button mold with s. c. with B. in each st. to end of mold, insert mold and dec. to center, close with sewing needle, fasten silk in edge of mold, * push up 4 inches of B. (2 inch L.), fasten in same st., sk. ¼ inch, * repeat. There are 9 L. around mold, sew mold to bottom of bag. Cut lining shape of bag, sl. st. around top of bag and fasten at bottom.

The AVONAY No. 610

Illustrated on page 25

A Striking Small Mouchoir Bag made of Glisten-
ing Steel Beads—Diamond Cut—and Large
in Size—The Unusual is their lightness to carry.

Made with HEMINWAY SILKS

Materials: No. 2249 Dark Brown, 2 spools Hampton Crochet Silk; 4 bunches Large Steel Beads; 1 Large Round Mold; 1 Steel Crochet Needle, No. 10.

Bottom of Bag: String beads (B.) on silk. Ch. 6, join in ring. **1st row.**—18 d. c. in ring, join each row with sl. st. **2nd row.**—3 d. c., * ch. 2, sk. 2, 3 d. c., * repeat to end of row, join. There are 6 sections of 3 d. c. **3rd row.**—3 d. c. over 3 d. c., ch. 2, s. c. with B. (silk over needle, insert needle in s. c., push B. toward needle, silk over needle, pull through all loops on needle), over ch. 2 of previous row, ch. 2, continue to end of row, always ch. 2 before and after each B. and group of 3 d. c. **4th row.**—3 d. c., ch. 2, s. c. with B., ch. 2, s. c. with B., ch. 2, repeat to end of row. Inc. each row in same manner until there are 9 B. in each section, join. S. c. with B. over center of 3 d. c., ch. 2, continue working round and round until bag measures 5¼ inches from the point. 1 row d. c. on top.

Beading: Ch. 5 for 1st d. tr. c., 3 more d. tr. c.,

* ch. 4, sk. 4, 4 d. tr. c. in next 4 sts., * continue around, join. 1 more row d. c.

Triple Picot: * 6 s. c. in 1st 6 sts., ch. 3, s. c. in same st., ch. 4, s. c. in same st., ch. 3, s. c. in same st. for picot, * repeat around, break silk.

Strings: Using 2 threads, ch. 25 inches, s. c. in 2nd ch. from needle, continue to end of ch. Make another string the same length and draw through beading from opposite sides of bag and fasten ends securely.

Covered Mold: With Brown, ch. 4, join in ring. **1st row.**—5 s. c. in ring. **2nd row.**—* 2 s. c. in 1st st., 1 s. c. in next st., * repeat. **3rd, 4th, 5th and 6th rows.**—Inc. in every 3rd st. of row. **7th row.**—Inc. every 4th st., insert mold and dec. to close button. Fasten silk in bottom of bag, string 4 B. and fasten in bottom of mold near center, run needle across ⅜ inch, string 3 more B., running through the 4th B. at bottom of bag, fasten well, back through same B., string 3 more and fasten well to button mold midway between the other 2 groups, ⅜ inch apart.

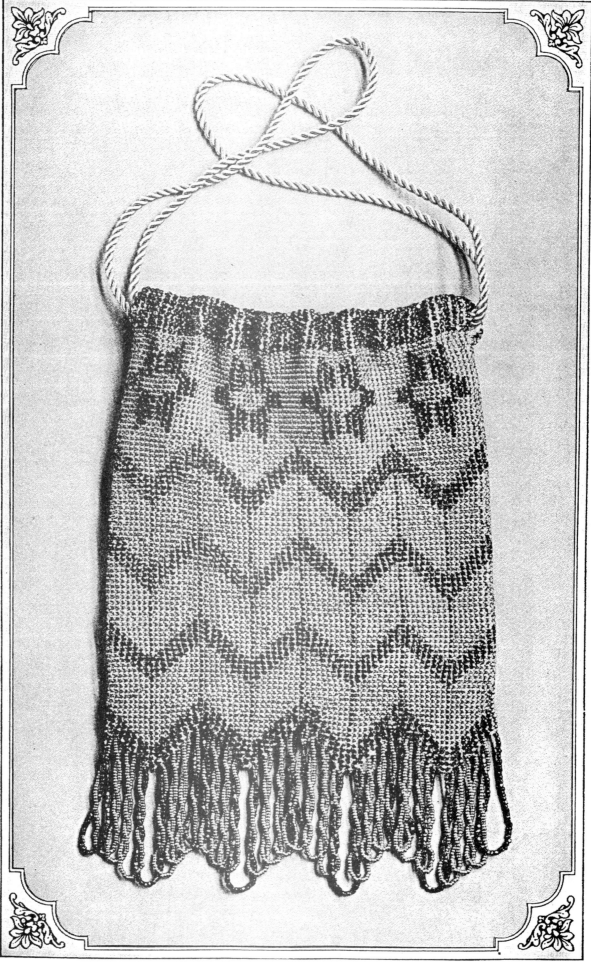

No. 607

LE TOUQUET No. 607

*A Knitted Bag of Over Seas Interest with Wavy Lines
of Dark Blue against Steel Background. The Star Border
is the Vanishing Point of the Outlines in Gold Beads.*

Made with HEMINWAY SILKS

Materials: No. 2304 Grey, 2 spools Purse Twist; 8 bunches No. 9 Round Steel Beads, 4 bunches No. 9 Round Gold Beads, 4 bunches Navy Iridescent Beads; ¼ yd. Satin or Silk for lining; 1 Pair No. 18 Steel Knitting Needles.

Top of Bag: String 1 bunch Navy Blue Beads (B.) on 1 spool silk, cast on 75 sts. and knit (kn.) 3 rows plain, which turns back at top when bag is made up. **1st row.**—Kn. 1 st., * insert needle in next st., push B. toward needle, complete st., * continue across row, turn. (Each row begins and ends with a plain kn. st.) **2nd row.**—Kn. back 1 row without B. Repeat 1st and 2nd rows 6 times more, this completes the border in Navy Blue B., break silk. (Size, 6¼ x 7¼ inches long.) **18th row.**—Start from point marked A on diagram and string upwards to the 17th row, then fasten silk and continue kn. as at beginning with 1 row plain always between B. rows, break silk and string B. from point B back to A, attach silk, working toward bottom of bag, continue in this manner, stringing 1 section at a time from C to B, D to C. and from E back to D, then when finishing the last section, kn. the 4 B. rows of diagram with plain rows between, this brings you to the dec. for points.

Divide sts. on needle in 4 sections for points and kn. each separately. Cast off the 1st and last st. of every row until 1 st. remains as shown in diagram. Complete a 2nd side, place the 2 right sides facing each other and sew or sl. st. together down sides and around points, turn.

Fringe: Attach silk directly on corner of bag, * string 4 inches Blue B. (2 inch loop), fasten ¼ inch down side of point, string 4 inches of Steel B., wind through 1st L. twice, fasten ¼ inch beyond; 2 more steel L. always winding twice in last L. made, * repeat from * to * 8 times more around points to opposite corner of bag. Cut lining same size of bag, sew up bottom and sides, place in position and sl. st. around top of bag just above the 1st B. row.

Casing for Cords: ¾ inch below top of bag, chain st. around on inside to form casing.

Cords: Using 3 threads, ch. 1, * silk over, insert needle in ch., silk over, pull L. through, silk over, pull through all L. on needle, * continue for 24 inches. Make a 2nd cord and draw through casing from opposite sides of bag, fasten neatly.

x NavyBlue beads
■ Gold beads
Background in steel beads shown by open mesh
/ One stitch silk.

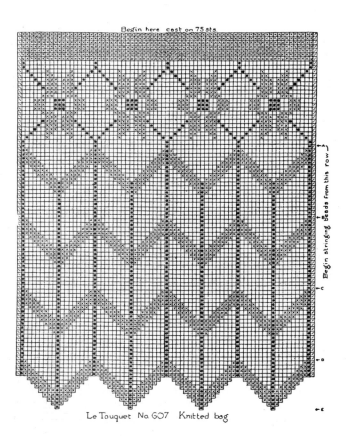

Begin here cast on 75 sts.

Begin stringing beads from this row

Le Touquet No. 607 Knitted bag

The SPHINX No. 604

Illustrated on cover

A Likeness Knitted in Beads and Silk of one of the Historical Strong Points of the Nile Country.

Made with HEMINWAY SILKS

Materials: No. 2000 Gold, 2 spools Purse Twist; 20 bunches Amber Glass Beads, 15 bunches Navy Glass Beads; ¼ yd. Gold Satin for Lining; 6 Brass Rings (½ inch diameter); 1 Pair No. 18 Steel Knitting Needles.

String 2 bunches of Navy Beads (B.) on 1 spool of Gold silk—as given in beginning of book.

Border at Top of Bag: Cast on 73 sts. Knit (kn.) 3 rows plain (size when completed, 7 inches wide, 9½ inches long from top to point of bag). Kn. 1 st. and insert needle in 2nd st., slip 1 B. and continue with 1 B. in each st. working across (½ of bag only as shown in illustration). **Next row.**—Kn. back plain. There is **always 1 plain row** of kn. between each B. row. Repeat these 2 rows 11 times more, break silk. **28th row.**—Begin the design in Amber and Blue, the plain knitted row is not shown in diagram. String B. very accurately from 1st horizontal bar at side, back to the 27th row, attach silk and kn. toward point, following the diagram closely, break silk and string from 2nd bar back to the 1st bar, attach silk, continue knitting.

Following the stringing and knitting of the successive bar sections to bottom of bag, complete a 2nd side, using care to keep of same measurement; sl. st. together on wrong side.

Fringe: Attach silk to corner of bag, string 4 inches of Blue B. (2 inch loop), fasten to bag with ⅛ inch space between, * string 4 inches of Amber B. for next L., twist through L. twice, fasten (¼ inch always beyond), string another 4 inch L., twist twice through L. last made, string 4 inches Blue B. for next L., twist twice through Amber L. just made, * repeat * to * around point to opposite side. Cut lining same shape of bag, sew up sides, place in bag and sl. st. around top.

Cover 6 brass rings (½ inch diameter) in s. c. with Gold Silk and sew ½ inch from top edge on inside of bag.

Cords: Cut 12 three-yard lengths of silk, twist tightly, double and twist again, repeat for 2nd cord and run through rings from opposite sides of bag, join by fancy knot.

The MIMI No. 617

Illustrated on page 18

Daintiest of the Small Wrist Vanity Bags—Pour La Jeune Fille.

Made with HEMINWAY SILKS

x Design in red beads
v Loop of 24 beads
iii Loop of 22 beads
/ Loop of 20 beads

Materials: No. 831 Grey, 1 spool Purse Twist, 4 bunches Red Glass Beads, ⅛ yd. Silk for lining, 1 Pair Steel Knitting Needles, No. 18.

Top of Bag: String 1 bunch of Beads (B.) on Purse Twist, cast on 42 sts. (Size, 3½ wide x 4 in. long, this does not include fringe at bottom.) Knit (kn.) 3 ridges (R.) plain, kn. 1, slip 24 B. for 1st loop (L.), kn. 3, continue across row (28 L. around, ¾ inch long), kn. back plain. Kn. plain to depth of fringe **already made** about 10 R. Kn. 1 st. plain and commence design slipping 1 B. in each st. checked in diagram, kn. back plain. Kn. 1 st., * slip 22 B. for 1st L. kn. 3 sts. plain. * repeat across row. Kn. 6 R. plain. Kn. 1 st., * slip 20 B., kn. 3 plain, * continue across row. Kn. 6 R. plain, casting off 1st st. both across and back on each row for dec. of bottom of bag. Kn. 1 st., slip 20 B. for first L., kn. 3, continue across. This forms fringe at bottom. Continue bag, reversing to row 1, casting on sts. where they were cast off. Sew up sides. Cut lining shape of bag allowing ½ inch **extra** at top for a small ¼ inch ruff and sl. st. at same time to top of bag, then ¼ inch below another running st. for casing.

Cords: Use about 5 threads 40 inches long, twist **tightly,** double and twist again, make a second one, **draw through casing from opposite sides of bag and join,** draw joining points through in casing.

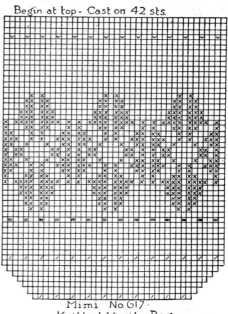

Begin at top- Cast on 42 sts.

Mimi No. 617
Knitted Vanity Bag

72 Stitches across - 117 ridges in length.

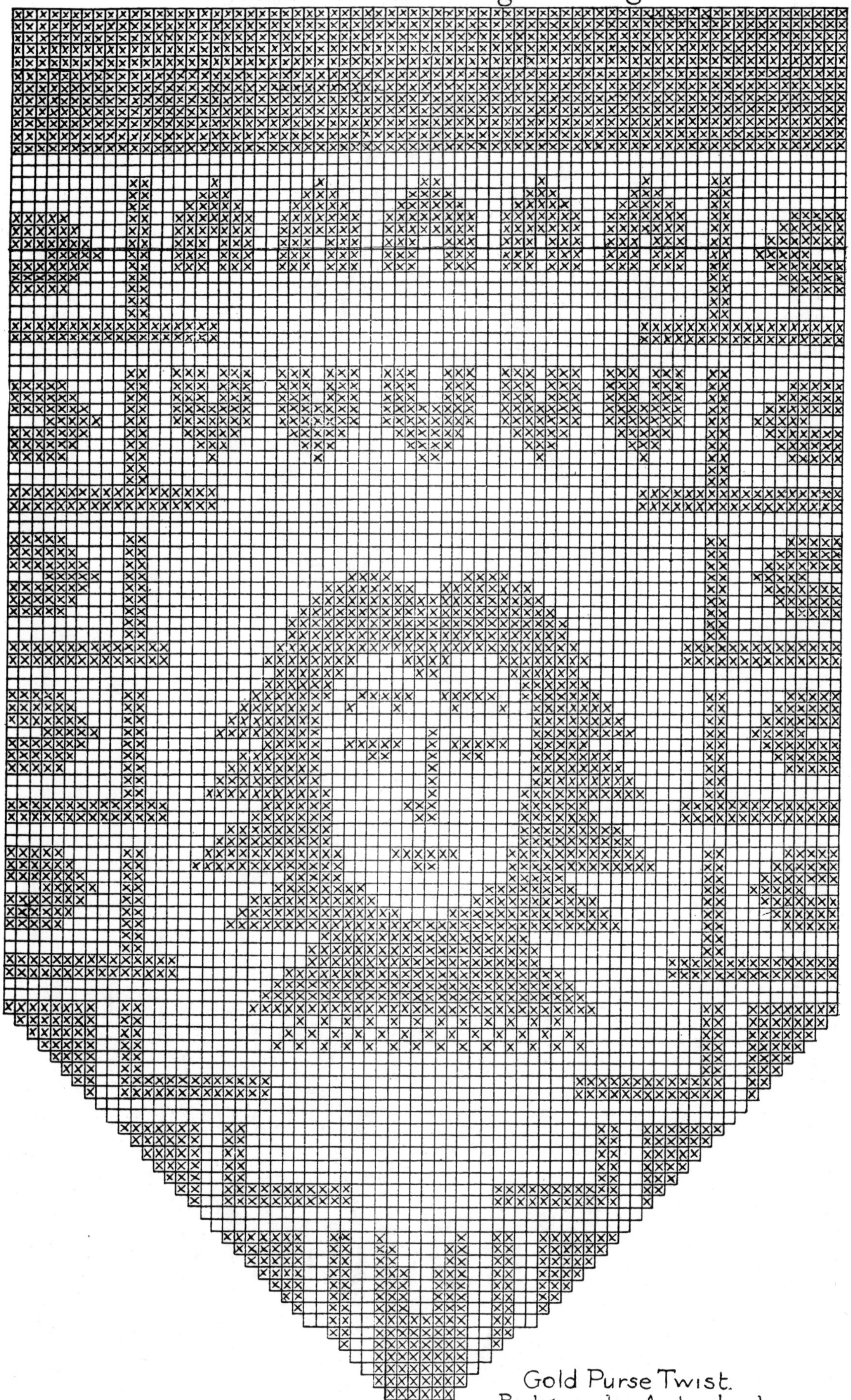

Sphinx Bag No 604

Gold Purse Twist.
Background in Amber beads
checked (x) design in navy blue beads

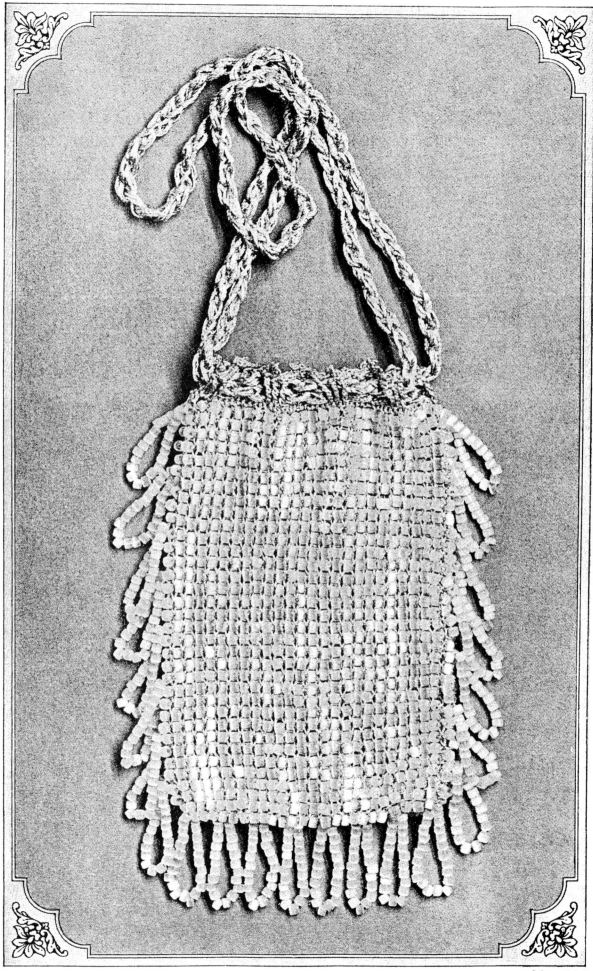

Elizabeth

BEAD WORK
BOOK

FIRST EDITION   PRICE 25 CENTS

Abbreviations and explanations of stitches:

Single Crochet ....S. C.
Skip ....Sk.
Double Crochet ....D. C.
Increase ....In.
Omit ....Om.
Plain ....Pl.
Space ....Sp.
Chain ....Ch.
Stitch ....St.

To increase put 2 st. in 1 with 1 bead in each.

To decrease skip 1 st.

———————

A few suggestions of designs.
Instructions—follow charts on page 3.

———————

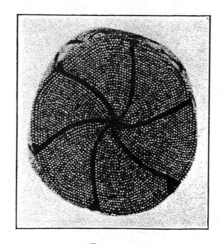

Figure 30

Figure 31

Instructions for Making Tassel:

String 2 bunches of beads on silk.
1. Ch. 3, join into ring.
2. Put 6 s. c. in ring.
3. Put 1 st. with bead in first st., 2 st. with bead in next for 6 rows.
4. Work plain, without increasing for 15 rows.
Put an 80-bead fringe in each st. at end.

Page two

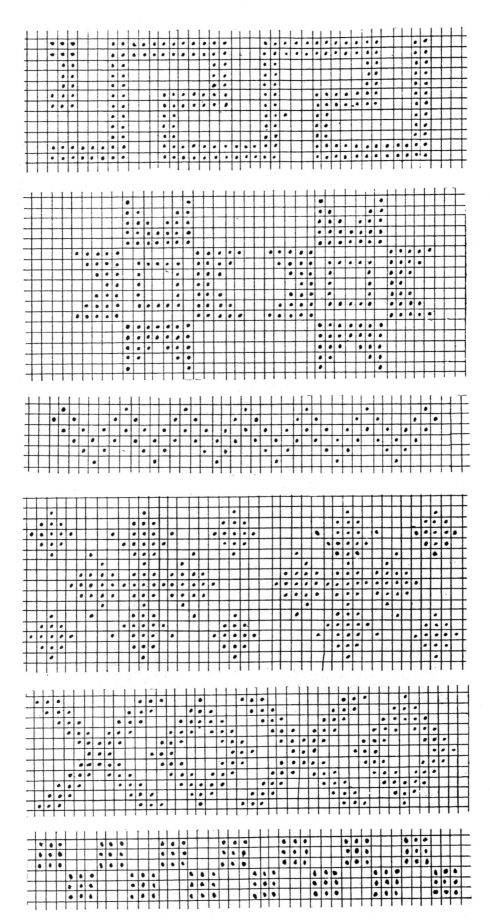

A few suggestions of designs.   *Page three*

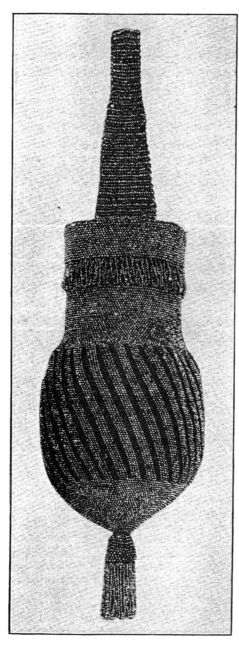

Bottle Shape Bag No. A-10

Materials:

3 spools Purse Twist, navy or white.

20 bunches cut steel beads or 30 bunches black jet beads.

1 steel hook, No. 9.

Instructions:

String two bunches of beads at a time.

1. Ch. 4, join into ring.

2. Put 6 s. c. in ring

3. Put 1 st. with bead in first st., and 2 st. with beads in next, for 4 rows.

4. One st. with bead in first st. and 2 st. with beads in every 5th st. and increase in this manner, until it measures 5½ inches in diameter, keeping it flat.

5. Work 4 st. with beads, 3 st. without for entire row, and continue in the same manner, one above the other for 4½ inches.

6. Continue work solid with beads in this manner; decrease 1 st. after each 10th bead, until there will be 120 beads left all around and make 29 rows in height.

7. Make 2½ inches plain, turn work from left to right, make a solid cuff of beads for 18 rows.

8. Put a 30-bead fringe at end of cuff.

9. For handle: Ch. 26 put 25 beads, and work 5 rows straight.

10. Decrease 1 st. at each side until there are 13 beads left. Work with 13 beads for 4½ inches, then increase same way as decreased, up to 26 st.

Sew on handle at each side of bag.

Instruction for tassel on page 2.

Fig. 30, from page 2, can be used for bottom of this bag.

Bag No. A-12
This attractive bag is made in two colors.

Materials:

2 spools Purse Twist, red.
1   "   "   grey.
12 bunches cut steel beads.   1 steel hook, No. 9.

Instructions:

String two bunches of beads at a time.
1. With red, Ch. 4, join into ring, put 6 s. c. in ring.
2. Put one st. with bead in every st., and 2 st. with beads
    in every 3rd st. to keep it flat, for 5 inches in diameter.
3. Make 2 st. with beads and 2 sp. for 3 rows.

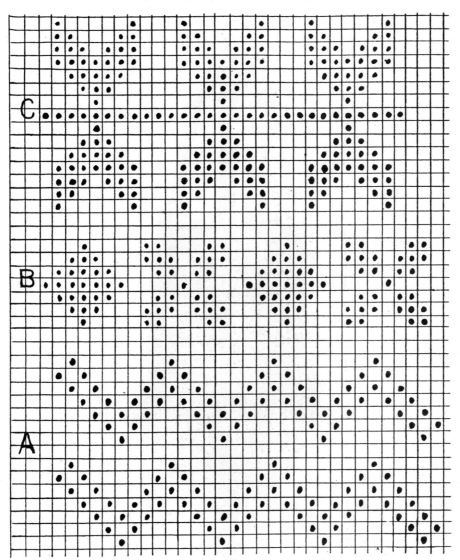

● beads   □ space

4. 3 st. with beads, 2 sp. for 4 rows.
5. 4 st. with beads, 2 sp. for 4 rows.
6. 2 rows pl. Then work according to chart A.
7. 2 rows pl.
8. With grey, work 1½ inches pl. and turn work from left to right and make cuff with design B; then put a fringe of 35 beads in every other st. at end of cuff.
9. With red, at top of cuff make 2 inches pl. and make cuff with design C, and put a 35-bead fringe in every other st. at end of cuff.
10. With grey at top of cuff below make 2½ inches pl., turn work from left to right, and repeat design B. Put a 35-bead fringe at end of cuff in every other st.

For Straps:

Ch. 9, turn, put 1 bead in every st. to have 8 st. across, and work for 9 inches. Make 2 straps, and sew on crossways on to bag. Instructions for tassel on page 2.

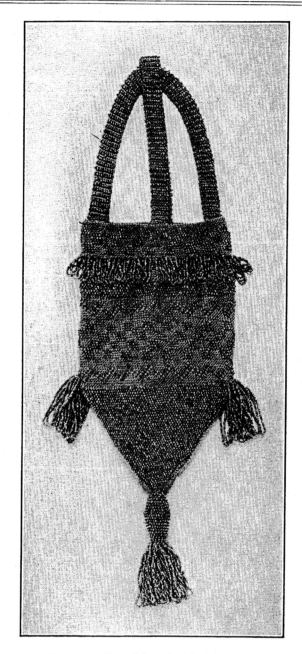

Bag No. A-14

This beautiful Misses, bag is worked from top down.

Materials:

 2 spools Purse Twist, grey.
 8 bunches cut steel beads or 12 bunches coral lustra beads.
 1 steel hook, No. 9.

Instructions:

String two bunches of beads at a time.
 1. Ch. 175, and join.
 2. Work pl. for 2 rows.
 3. Put 1 bead in every st. for 10 rows.

Page eight

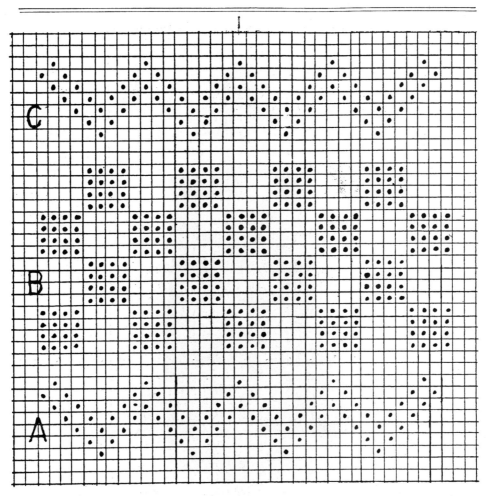

● beads
□ space

4. 2 rows pl.

5. Work according to charts C, B and A.

6. 2 rows pl. without beads.

7. Work 4 rows with beads straight, and then decrease 1 st. at each side until there is 6 st. left.

8. Begin at top again; make 1½ inches pl., turn work from left to right, and work cuff same as chart B.

9. Then put a 30-bead fringe on cuff.

10. Make 1 tassel for each side, as illustrated, one larger for the bottom.

For Straps:

Ch. 9, put 8 beads and work for 10 inches. Make two straps and sew on to bag crossways.

Instruction for tassel on page 2.

Bag No. A-16

An attractive, newly-designed bag, and very easy to make.

Materials:

    4 spools Purse Twist, black.

    15 bunches cut steel beads or 25 bunches blue iris beads.

    1 steel hook, No. 9.

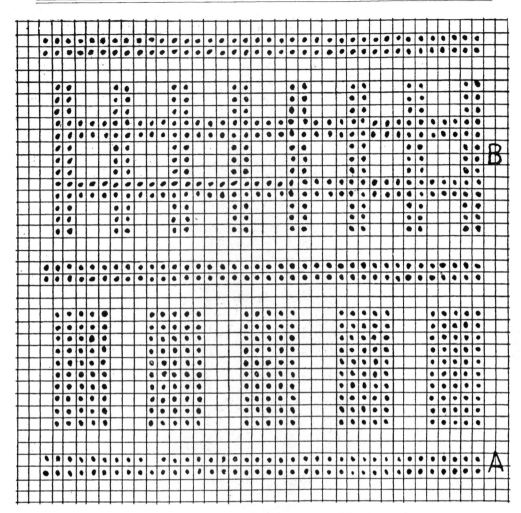

● beads
□ space

Instructions:

String 2 bunches beads at a time.

1. Ch. 4, join into ring. Make 6 s. c. in same ring.
2. Put 1 bead in first st., 2 pl. in next st., having 6 sections; 1 bead in each, 2 sp. between.
3. Increase 1 bead at each row in every section until there are 35 beads in every section, having 2 sp. between each.
4. Then work according to charts AA on page 20.
5. 2 rows pl. and work charts A and B.
6. Repeat chart A.
7. Make 2½ inches pl., skipping 5 st. in every row of the first 4 rows.
8. Turn work from left to right and make design on cuff from chart B.
9 Put a 40-bead fringe in every other st. at the end of the cuff.

A large stuffed tassel trims the bag nicely.
Instructions for tassel on page 2.

Page eleven

Bag No. A-18

This seamless square bag can be used for opera glasses, as well as for other purposes, can also be made in a smaller size, and different desirable shades.

Materials:

3 spools Purse Twist, black.
10 bunches cut steel beads.
1 steel hook, No. 9.

Instructions:

String 2 bunches of beads at a time.
1. Ch. 75 and work around ch. for 4 rows pl.
2. Put 1 bead in every stitch for 14 rows, then follow charts A, B and C.
3. Make 2½ inches pl., turn work from left to right, make design on cuff from chart B.
4. Put on a 50-bead fringe in every other st. at the end of cuff, and a 70-bead fringe on the bottom.

A sterling silver chain matches bag nicely.

Page twelve

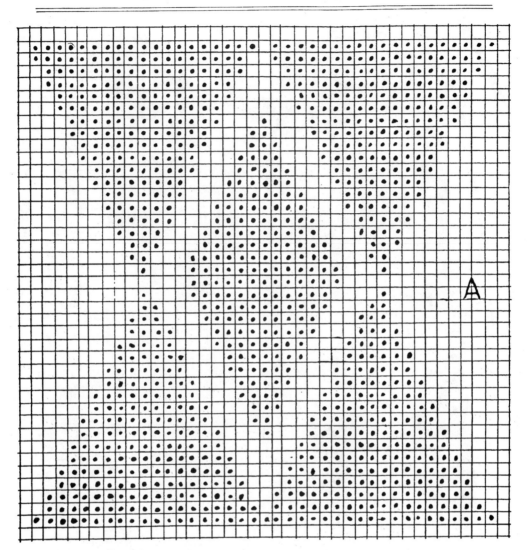

• beads
□ space

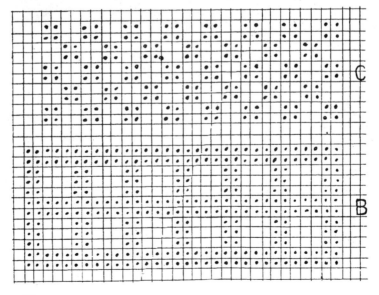

□ space
• beads

THE NOVELTY AND SIMPLICITY IN BEAD BAGS
Red Bead Bag No. 2

Materials required: 1 spool Purse Twist, 5 bunches of beads, 1 pair steel knitting needles.

Directions: Cast on 46 sts., hold the two needles together and cast on sts. on this, then pull one needle out. In coming back slip a bead after each st. Knit next row plain. Continue beading on one side till there are 7 rows of beads.

There are 1 st. and 1 bead on either edge the full length of bag. There are 2 sts. between the panels of beads.

If the bag is to be mounted on a frame, leave 1 bead off on edges for first 15 ridges to sew into frame. Remembering 1 st. on edges and 2 between panels of beads. Slip beads according to the following:

RIDGES	BEADS
4	1-2-2-2-2-2, 1 st. on end
5	1-3-2-3-2-3, 1 st. on end
7	1-4-2-4-2-4, 1 st. on end
8	1-5-2-5-2-5, 1 st. on end
9	1-6-2-6-2-6, 1 st. on end
20	1-7-2-7-2-7, 1 st. on end

53 Ridges—One-half of bag.

Always increase or decrease width of bag by **4** sts. One row is knitted plain, the other beaded the entire length of bag.

The sides are either sewed or crocheted together.

Bag No. A-20

This Seamless Envelope bag can be made in various combinations of colored and steel beads, with silk to match.

Materials:

2 spools Purse Twist, grey.
4 bunches cut steel beads.
4 bunches Royal Blue cut steel beads.
1 steel hook, No. 9.

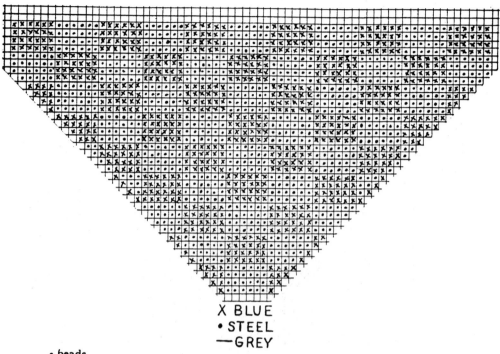

X BLUE
• STEEL
—GREY

• beads
[ ] space

Instructions:

String 1 bunch of steel beads on spool.
1. Ch. 75.
2. Work all around ch. for 4 rows, increasing 1 st. on each side, then work as follows:
3. 8 rows of steel beads.
4. 2 rows pl.
5. 8 rows Royal Blue beads.
6. 2 rows pl. and work so until there are 4 stripes of each color.
7. Make 5 rows pl. without beads.

For Flap:

String 6 beads of each color on silk, and work from one side of the bag to the other, according to chart. Sew on a 50-bead loop fringe all around flap and an 80-bead fringe of Royal Blue around bottom.

For Straps:

Ch. 12, put eleven beads and work for 8 inches, sew on at each side of bag.

A small piece of wire from one end of the flap to the other will hold the bag straight.

Bag No. A-22

Unusually attractive bag of imported red cut steel beads.

Materials:

3 spools Purse Twist, navy.
12 bunches red cut steel beads.
1 steel hook, No. 9.

Instructions:

String 2 bunches of beads at a time.
1. Ch. 4, join into ring, 6 s. c. in ring.

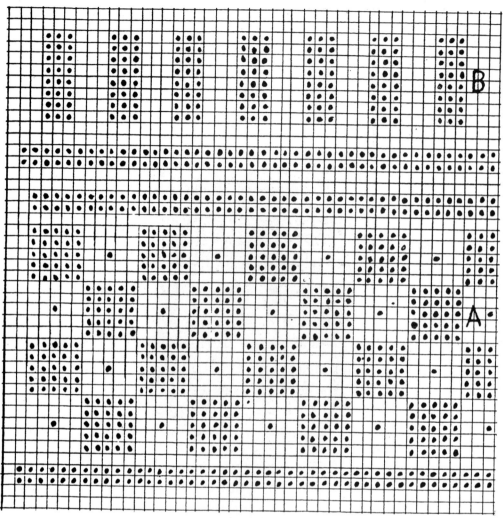

• beads   □ space

2. Put 1 st. with bead in each of the first 2 st. and 2 st. with beads in next st. and continue working in the same manner until there are 40 beads around the circle keeping it flat.

3. 1 row pl.

4. Make 2 st. with beads, one without, for 3 rows.

5. Increase until there are 11 beads in every section with 1 pl. between.

6. 2 rows pl., 2 rows with beads, repeat same for 3 times. Then follow charts A and B.

7. 2 rows of beads.

8. 2 rows pl. and repeat chart B.

9. Make 2½ inches pl., decreasing 4 st. in each of the first 4 rows.

10. Turn work from left to right, and make cuff from chart A. Put a 30-bead fringe at end of cuff.

A bronze chain with rings is suitable for this bag.

Instructions for tassel see page 2.

Bag No. A-24

This attractive bag can be made in various shades.

Materials:

4 spools Purse Twist, navy.
18 bunches cut steel beads or bronze iris beads.
1 steel hook, No. 9.

Instructions:

String 2 bunches of beads at a time.
1. Ch. 4, join into ring. Put 6 s. c. in ring.
2. Put 1 st. with bead in every st., and 2 st. with beads in every third st. for 4 rows.
3. 1 row pl.
4. Put 1 bead in the first st. and 1 pl. in the next for 2 rows.

Page eighteen

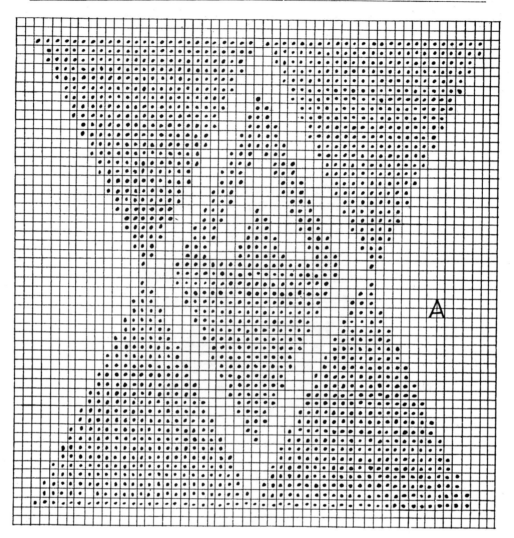

• beads   □ space

5. Increase 1 bead in every bead section, having 2 beads and 1 sp. between, for 2 rows.
6. Increase 1 bead, having 3 beads and 1 sp. between, for 2 rows, and increase so until there are 11 beads in every section, 1 sp. between.
7. Omit the first bead in every section, having 2 sp. between instead of 1, until there are 5 sp.
8. Put 1 bead in the center of each sp. section having 2 sp. at each side, still omitting the first bead.
9. Work until there are 3 beads in center and decrease back to 1.
10. 2 rows pl., and follow charts A—B and C on page 20.
11. 2 rows pl., 1 row with beads.
12. 1 row pl, 1 row with beads.

For Laps:

Divide all stitches from top of bag into 8 sections, having 4 laps and 4 sp. in between. Work each lap separately, decreasing 1 st. at each side until there are 3 beads left; then put a 50-bead tassel on each lap. Make 1 large tassel for bottom.
Instructions for tassel on page 2.

Page nineteen

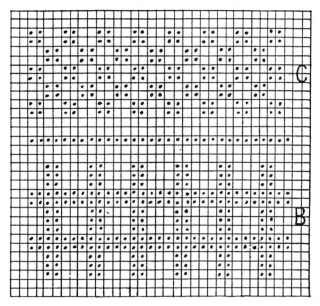

For Bag, No. A-24, on page 18

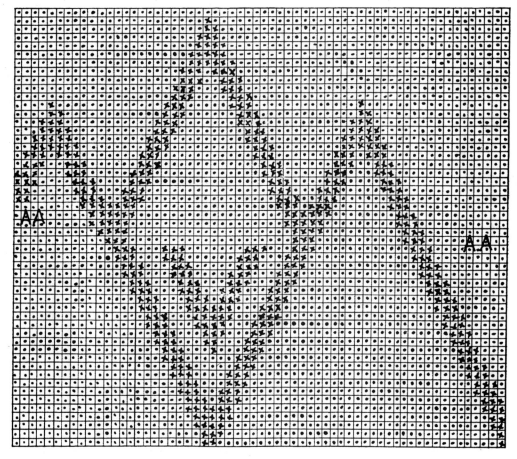

Chart for Bag No. A-16 on page 10.

• beads
x space

Page twenty

A Charming Collection

of

M O D E R N

Beaded Bags

Combining simplicity of Design,
with smart and refined appearance.

*Complete and simple
directions for making with
photographs and charts.*

COPYRIGHT 1924 by

DRITZ-TRAUM CO.

258 FIFTH AVENUE, NEW YORK, N.Y.

SOLE
DISTRIBUTORS
OF
HIAWATHA
LEADS
BAG FRAMES
NOVELTIES

FOREWORD

IT is not at all surprising that the vogue of making beaded bags is so great, when one can realize the possibility of creating things of exquisite beauty with a few beads and some silk thread.

The art of making beaded bags until recently, was a complicated and tedious task, attempted only by the early American Indians in this country, and the mountain peasants of the old world, who from childhood were trained by their parents and grandparents.

With this little book as a guide it is merely a pleasant divergence to blend sparkling beads with silk, and also enables one to possess that beautiful adjunct that is so necessary to complete Milady's costume.

In order to obtain the proper results, care should be used in selecting beads. They should be of enduring color and lustre, properly cut, uniform in size and quality. "Hiawatha" beads are selected for these requisites and are therefore recommended. "Hiawatha" bag frames and bag cords are also made of the finest materials obtainable and give absolute satisfaction.

Colors:– The selection of colors is an important consideration, and by following these suggestions satisfactory results will be obtained.

Self Colors:— In this group it is merely necessary to match the beads with the thread used, viz.—black with black, blue with blue, red with red, etc., etc.

Contrasting Colors:—In making a bag of contrasting shades, opaque beads should be used. Black or Navy thread combined with steel beads always effects a pleasing contrast. Here is recommended the new "Hiawatha Platinum" steel plated beads, which with ordinary care will not tarnish. Black thread combined with red or white beads or vice-versa, grey with jet, etc., produce proper contrasting effects.

Blended Colors:—This group affords the opportunity of producing individuality. Silk thread being opaque, transparent beads should be used so that the color of the beads will absorb the color of the thread and blend together. Light amber colored beads combined with brown thread will produce a shade in between the two. Purple beads combined with violet thread, light and medium blue beads with grey or other shades of blue thread, etc., always blend well.

There are several kinds of beads amongst the "Hiawatha" collection, the colors which are difficult to describe. They are known as gold irridescent lustres and transparent irridescent beads. Radiant shades, such as golden brown, jade green, violet, etc., are blended with tints of translucent gold in the same bead. These truly make gorgeous bags.

MODEL 116

HIAWATHA

ABBREVIATIONS USED IN THIS BOOK

B.	Bead or Beads	P.H.S.	Plain Half Stitch
CH.	Chain	PL.	Plain
Cr.	Crochet	R.	Ridge
H. St.	Half Stitch	SLD.	Slide
K.	Knit	ST.	Stitch
L.	Line		

"THE WELLESLEY" No. 116

Materials: 20 Bchs. "Hiawatha" cut beads 9/0.
2 spools purse twist
1 Pair "Hiawatha" knitting pins size 17.
1 Pair "Hiawatha" knitting pin protectors.
1 "Hiawatha" drawstring cord No. 725.

This model made with black purse twist and crystal gems No. 21/9 looks particularly well.

Size of Bag: Width 5½ inches—length 6½ inches.

This bag is made in 7 vertical patterns of bead slides in diamond shapes and graduated stripes with plain knitting between the patterns as follows:

Cast on 63 St.—K. 1 R. (ridge) Pl. K. 8 R. with 1 B. in each St., always coming back with Pl. St. (No beads) on inside of bag.

10th R. K. 1 Pl. K. 2 B. K. 1 Pl. Slide Pattern 1 (see table below). K. 1 Pl. K. 2 B. * K. 2 Pl. K. 2 B. K. 1 Pl. Slide Pattern 2 (starting diamond).

K. 1 Pl. K. 2 B. K. 2 Pl. K. 2 B. K. 1 Pl. Slide Pattern 3. K. 1 Pl. K. 2 B. *. Repeat from * to * 2 more times and finish with 1 Pl. St.

Note: When knitting back on inside of bag to complete the ridge, always knit plain except when sliding beads.

Note that balance of bag is made exactly as the 10th ridge with the execution of the patterns which are made in the following manner:

Vertical Patterns 2-4-6 are for Diamond Shapes.

** On	1st	R.—Slide 1 B.
"	2nd	R.— " 2 B.
"	3rd	R.— " 3 B.
"	4th	R.— " 4 B.
"	5th	R.— " 5 B.
"	6th	R.— " 6 B.
"	7th	R.— " 7 B.
"	8th	R.— " 8 B.
"	9th	R.— " 8 B.
"	10th	R.— " 8 B.
"	11th	R.— " 7 B.
"	12th	R.— " 6 B.
"	13th	R.— " 5 B.
"	14th	R.— " 4 B.
"	15th	R.— " 3 B.
"	16th	R.— " 2 B.
"	17th	R.— " 1 B.**

This completes 1 full diamond. Repeat from ** to ** until 9 diamonds are finished.

Note: Slides No. 2-4-6 are exactly the same.

Vertical Patterns 1-3-5-7 are for Graduated Stripes

***On	1st to 9th	R.—Slide 2 B.
"	10th to 20th	R.— " 3 B.
"	21st to 31st	R.— " 4 B.
"	32nd to 44th	R.— " 5 B.
"	45th to 57th	R.— " 6 B.
"	58th to 68th	R.— " 7 B.
"	69th to 80th	R.— " 8 B.***

This completes the graduated stripe for ½ the bag. Repeat from *** to *** in reverse order for the other half of bag.

Note: Slides No. 1-3-5-7 are exactly the same.

Tabs: Cast on 9 St. * K. 1 Pl. K. 7 B. K 1 Pl. coming back with a line of plain in the back *. Repeat from * to * until tab measures 2 inches. Make 8 tabs. Attach tabs to bag, 4 on each side, leaving 1 end loose on each.

Lining & Mounting: Sew up sides of bag. Line bag with piece of silk and attach drawstring cord, and sew up loose ends of tabs. Then sew 4 loops 3 inches long on each side at top of bag.

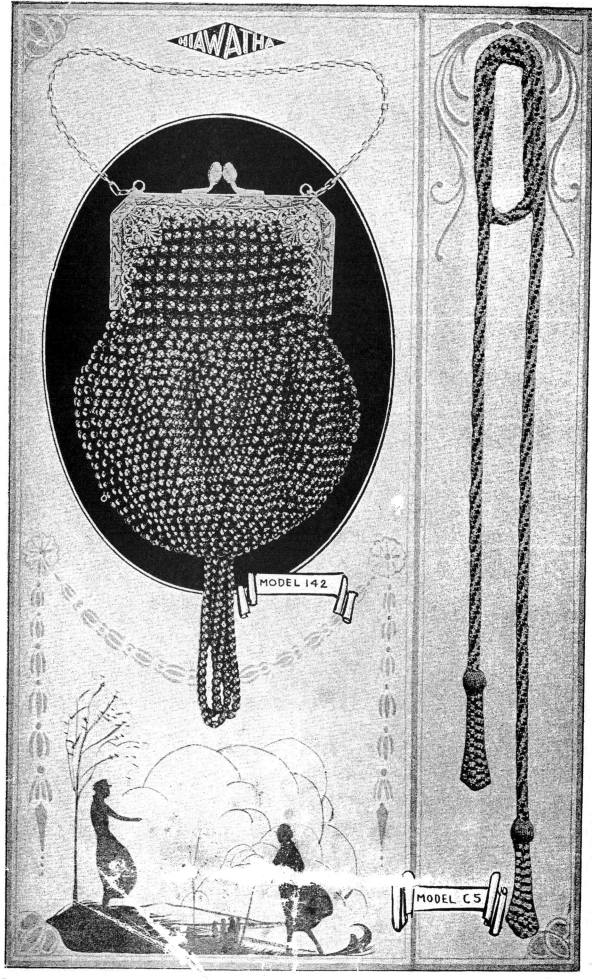

MODEL 142

MODEL C5

"THE SILVER-GLO" No. 142

Materials: 4 Bchs. "Hiawatha" Silver-Glo Gems No. 3117.
1 spool Purse twist.
1 "Hiawatha" steel crochet hook No. 9.
1 "Hiawatha" Filigree Frame No. 5888/4.

Silver-Glo Gems come in a large variety of colors that can be blended into the most beautiful shades.

Size of Bag: Width at top 4 inches—Bottom 5¼ inches—Length 6¼ inches.

Pattern stitch used throughout the bag (3 chain, 1 B. 1 H. St.)

Chain 8 and join to form a ring. Fill in with 28 P. H. S. Then Cr. 3 chain St. with 1 B. in every other H. St.

Continue working around circle increasing 7 B. in each row for 22 rows, keeping the work flat and even.

Top:—23rd row: Continue without any increase, gathering in the previous row evenly and carefully. Decrease the bag gradually in the next 2 rows until the circumference measures 11 inches.

26th row: Work one-half of the circle (22 beads) then turn bag and make 1 row of Pl. St. (3 chain), turn again and make 1 row with B. Continue alternating 1 row Pl. and 1 row of B. decreasing 1 St. at each end. Make about 6 rows of B. in this way until top fits frame. It is best to decrease the Pl. rows to get an even graduation.

Tassel: Attach thread to centre at bottom of bag and string 6 inches of B. (making a 3 inch loop). Make 4 loops.

Lining and Mounting: Line bag with piece of silk and attach frame

---

"VANITY FAIR" No. 141

Illustrated on page 26

Materials: 12 Bchs. "Hiawatha" Radium Lustre Beads No. 2720.
1 Spool Purse Twist.
1 "Hiawatha" steel crochet hook No. 9.
1 "Hiawatha" Jeweled Frame No. 5927.

Use Radium Lustre beads No. 2720 in the color to match the jewels on the frame.

Size of bag: 3½ inches in diameter.

Chain 8 and join to form a ring. Fill in with 12 H. St.

Cr. 2 H. St. with B., 1 Pl., 2 H. St. with B., 1 Pl.
2 H. St. with B., 1 Pl., 2 H. St. with B., 1 Pl.
2 H. St. with B., 1 Pl., 2 H. St. with B., 1 Pl.

On the next row Cr. 3 H. St. with B., 1 Pl., etc., until end of line. Continue in this manner increasing 1 B. in each section until you have 22 B. in each section. Then Cr. 3 rows of Pl. St. (No beads). This completes one side of bag. Make the other side in exactly the same manner.

Tassel: Chain 8 and join to form a ring. Fill in with 12 H. St., Cr. around with H. St. and B. increasing 1 B. in each row for 12 rows. Then Cr. a 5 inch loop (2½ inches doubled) in every other st.

Handle: Chain 7 to start. Cr 1 row H. St. Plain, and 1 row H. St. with B., and back 1 row Pl. etc., until handle measures 8 inches.

Line bag with silk and make a pocket at the bottom of each half. Attach each half of bag to sides of frame. Line handle with piece of silk and attach to top of frame and to little ring provided for that purpose in the centre of hinge at bottom of bag.

MODEL C5 *described on page 13*

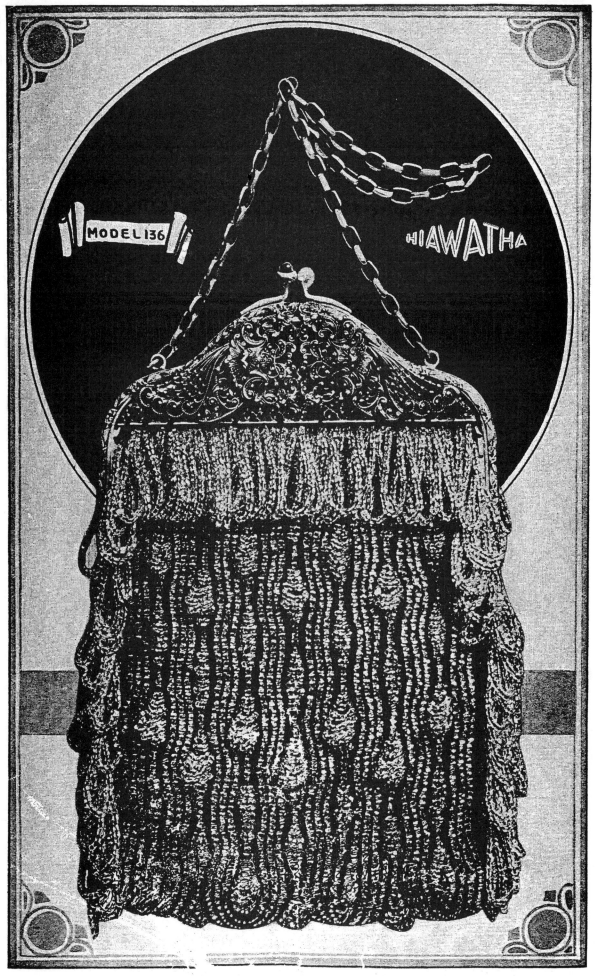

Model 136

Hiawatha

"THE MANDALAY"
Model No. 136

Materials: 20 Bchs. "Hiawatha" Crystal Gems No. 21/9.
1 spool purse twist.
1 pair "Hiawatha" steel knitting pins No. 17.
1 pair "Hiawatha" knitting pin protectors.
1 "Hiawatha" 5-inch filigree frame No. 5896.

A distinctive bag made with **Crystal Gems No. 21/9 on a dark background.**

Size of Bag: Width 5 inches—length 6 inches.

Cast on 58 St. K. 2 R. (ridges) Pl. without B. (2 rows make 1 ridge).

3rd row: * K. 1 Pl. K. 1 St. with 2 inches of B. to form a loop. * Repeat from * to * across bag making a row of loop fringes.

The balance of this bag is made in 7 vertical patterns of bead slides in diamond shapes with plain knitting between the patterns as follows:

4th Ridge—K. 4 Pl. K. 3 B. K. 2 Pl. Sld. Pattern 1 (see table below). K. 2 Pl. K. 3B. K. 2 Pl. Sld. Pattern 2. K. balance of ridge in the same manner, making patterns 3-5 & 7 same as pattern 1, and patterns 4-6 same as pattern 2. Finish with 4 Pl. St.

The following table shows how many beads to slide in every ridge for each pattern:

Vertical Patterns No. 1-3-5-7.			Vertical Patterns No. 2-4-6		
4th— 5th R.—Slide	1	B.	4th R.—Slide	8	B.
6th— 7th R.— "	2	B.	5th R.— "	7	B.
8th—11th R.— "	3	B.	6th R.— "	5	B.
12th—13th R.— "	2	B.	7th R.— "	3	B.
14th—15th R.— "	1	B.	8th R.— "	2	B.
16th—17th R.— "	1	B.	9th—10th R.— "	1	B.
18th R.— "	2	B.	11th—12th R.— "	1	B.
19th R.— "	3	B.	13th—14th R.— "	2	B.
20th R.— "	5	B.	15th—18th R.— "	3	B.
21st R.— "	7	B.	19th—20th R.— "	2	B.
22nd R.— "	8	B.	21st—22nd R.— "	1	B.
23rd R.— "	7	B.	23rd—24th R.— "	1	B.
24th R.— "	5	B.	25th R.— "	2	B.
25th R.— "	3	B.	26th R.— "	3	B.
26th R.— "	2	B.	27th R.— "	5	B.
27th—28th R.— "	1	B.	28th R.— "	7	B.

Note that patterns 1-3-5-7 are exactly the same.

Note that patterns 2-4-6 are exactly the same.

29th to 52nd R. Repeat from 4th to 28th Ridges.

53rd to 76th R. Repeat from 4th to 28th Ridges.

This completes one-half the bag. Make the other half in exactly the same manner in reverse order.

Sew up sides of bag, leaving enough space open at top for frame.

Loops on side of bag are made by stringing 1½ inches of beads double, to form a loop ther from bottom to top of bag. Make a lo side of bag, leaving a small space between the two rows.

Line bag with piece of silk an attach frame.

HIAWATHA

MODEL 135

"THE NIAGARA"
Model No. 135

Materials: 20 Bchs. "Hiawatha" cut beads 9/0.
2 spools purse twist.
1 "Hiawatha" steel crochet hook No. 9.
1 "Hiawatha" Filigree Frame No. 5863.

A striking combination is obtained by using the new Opalescent Gems No. 23/9 with old gold purse twist. Original model made with Black Purse twist and "Hiawatha" Porcelain chalk beads No. 84.

Size of Bag: Width 5 inches. Length 6 inches.

Start with 66 chain St., **2nd to 11th rows.** Cr. on each side of chain P. H. S. Continue Cr. around bag in this manner making 10 rows of P. H. S.

12th row: Cr. 1 B. then 1 loop (long enough to cover rows of plain stitches beneath). Continue across, making 10 loops. Cr. 26 P. H. S. (no beads). Cr. 1 loop (as before) 1 B., etc., making 20 loops. Cr. 26 P. H. S. (no beads). Repeat 1 loop, 1 B., etc., making 10 loops.

13th to 22nd rows: Same as 2nd to 11th rows.

23rd row: Same as 12th row.

24th to 33rd rows: Same as 2nd to 11th rows.

34th row: Cr. 1 B. 1 loop (as before), etc., making 10 loops. Cr. 12 P. H. S. Cr. 2 loops 3½ inches long. 12 P. H. S. Then 1 loop, 1 B., etc., making 20 loops. 12 P. H. S. and 2 loops 3½ inches long. 12 P. H. S. 1 loop, 1 B., etc., making 10 loops. Continue crocheting design, using the illustrated chart as a guide.

Lining and Mounting: Attach bag frame and line bag with silk.

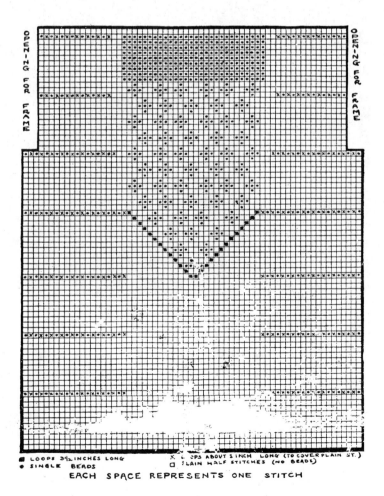

■ LOOPS 3½ INCHES LONG   X LOOPS ABOUT 1 INCH LONG (TO COVER PLAIN ST.)
● SINGLE BEADS   □ PLAIN HALF STITCHES (NO BEADS)

EACH SPACE REPRESENTS ONE STITCH

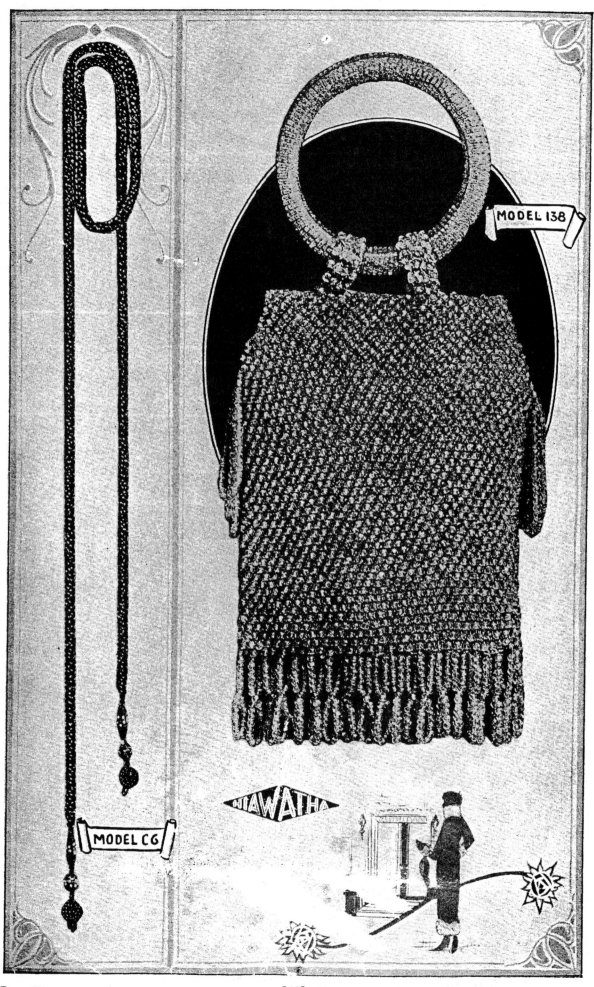

MODEL 138

MODEL C G

HIAWATHA

"THE MIGNONETTE" No. 138

Materials: 6 Bchs. "Hiawatha" crystallized gems No. 3129.
1 Spool Purse Twist.
1 "Hiawatha" Steel Crochet Hook No. 9.
1 Pair "Hiawatha" beaded rings No. 3137.

Made with a new bead in size that can be had in unusually brilliant shades—specially adapted for making all kinds of bags and chains.

Size of Bag: Width at top 4½ inches—width at bottom 5 inches. Length 6 inches.

Pattern stitch used throughout the bag (2 chain, 1 bead, 1 half stitch).

Start with about 60 chain St. or 5 inches long. Cr. all around Ch. with P. H. S. (no beads). Then Cr. 2 Ch. St. with 1 B. in every other H. St. Continue Cr. around bag in this manner until 37 rows of B. are finished.

Top: * crochet back and forth on one side of bag. Make 11 rows of B., decreasing 1 St. at each end about every third row.* Repeat from * to * for other side of bag.

Tabs: Start with 6 Ch. St. Cr. 1 row P. H. S. Then Cr. 4 B., using the same St. as used in rest of bag. Cr. 8 rows of B. in this manner—make 4 tabs.

Fringe: String 21 B. and go back through the 7th B. from the top. String 6 more B. and fasten to bag. Repeat 20 times. **Tassels** on side of bag are made by stringing 4 inches of B. (which makes a 2 inch loop) and attaching right under opening at side of bag. Make 3 loops on each side.

Line bag with piece of silk, putting a piece of stiff buckram between lining and beadwork at top of bag, where sides are open.

Sew 2 tabs on each side at top of bag, leaving 1 end loose, insert beaded rings and sew down loose ends of tabs.

"THE NOTRE DAME" No. C6

Materials: 3 Bchs. "Hiawatha" Crystallized Gems No. 3129.
1 "Hiawatha" Steel Crochet Hook No. 10.
50 Yards Buttonhole Twist or Tatting Thread.
2 Beaded Balls No. 2523.
2 Pcs. each of "Hiawatha" Real Venetian Beads, round and oblong.

The crocheting on this chain is done exactly the same as chain No. 1, except that there are 4 beads in a row instead of 6. (See page 29.)
Tassels: Attach tassels as illustrated.

THE FRENCH SCARF CHAIN No. C5

Illustrated on page 6

Materials: 2 Bchs. "Hiawatha" Silver Glo Gems No. 3117.
2 Bchs. "Hiawatha" Cut Crystallized Gems No. 3129.
2 Beaded Balls No. 2523.
50 Yards Buttonhole Twist.
1 "Hiawatha" Steel Crochet Hook No. 10.
2 "Hiawatha" Beading Needles.

The important part of making this model is the stringing of the beads. String 1 round bead and 1 cut bead alternately—½ bunch of each at a time. Crochet in the same manner as chain No. 1 with the exception that there are 4 beads in a row. (See page 29.)

Length 60 inches—attach 1 beaded ball at each end and a tassel of 5 strings of beads 4 inches long.

MODEL 125

HIAWATHA

"THE FAN-TAN" No. 125

Materials: 12 Bchs. "Hiawatha" quality beads size 9/0.
    1 spool purse twist.
    2 "Hiawatha" steel knitting pins No. 17.
    1 Pair "Hiawatha" Knitting Pin protectors.
    1 "Hiawatha" bag frame No. 5935.

A good combination is obtained by using grey silk and red transparent-irridescent beads No. 1105.

Size of bag: 5 inches wide at top—6 inches long.

Cast on 48 St. K. 1 ridge Pl. (2 rows make 1 ridge). K. 4 ridges with 1 B. in each St. always coming back with a line of Pl. (without beads) on inside of bag. K. 3 Pl. St. at the end of each row.

11th R. K. 3 Pl. * Slide 1 B. K. 5 Pl. * Repeat from * to * 8 times, making 9 diamonds in all across bag. Finish line with 3 Pl. St. K. the next line in the same manner, sliding 2 beads instead of 1. Continue this way, increasing the slides in every line until there are 8B. slides. This completes ½ the diamond. Repeat in reverse order for the other half of the diamond.

26th-27th R.: K. 1 B. in each St. across line, starting and finishing with 3 Pl. St. at each end.

28th R.: K. 3 Pl. ** Slide 1 B. K. 5 Pl. ** Repeat from ** to ** 8 times, making 9 slides in all. Finish line with 3 Pl St.

K. the following R. in the same manner, increasing the slides as follows:

2 Ridges Slide 2 Beads	5 Ridges Slide 5 Beads
3 Ridges Slide 3 Beads	6 Ridges Slide 6 Beads
4 Ridges Slide 4 Beads	21 Ridges Slide 7 Beads

This completes one-half the bag. For the other half repeat in reverse order. Sew up sides of bag, leaving an opening at the top to fit frame.

Line with piece of silk and attach frame.

"THE BERKELEY" No. 143

Illustrated on page 27

Materials: 18 Bchs. "Hiawatha" Cut Beads No. 2719 size 6/0.
    3 Spools Purse Twist.
    1 "Hiawatha" Steel Crochet Hook No. 9.
    1 "Hiawatha" Draw string Cord No. 617 or 725.

Original model made with large lustre beads No. 2719 which can be had in a variety of beautiful colors.

Size of Bag: Width 5¾ inches. Length 7½ inches.

1st row: Chain 133 to start.

2nd row: Cr. all around ch. 1 row P.H.S.

3rd row: Cr. alternately 5 B. and 2 P.H.S. all around.

4th row: Cr. over the 1st B. in the 3rd row 1 P.H.S. then Cr. 5 B. 2 P. H. S., 5 B. etc., etc., until end of line.

Continue in this manner always putting 1 P.H.S. over the 1st B. in the previous row until 79 rows are crocheted.

Inverted Cuff: Reverse work and join thread.

1st row: Cr. 1 B. in every other St. all around.

2nd row: Cr. 1 B. in every other St., the B. to be where the space is on 1st row.

3rd, 4th, 5th rows: Cr. 3 rows P.H.S. all around.

6th row: Cr. 1 B., 7 P. H. S., 1 B., 7 P. H. S., etc., all around.

7th row: Cr. 3 B., 5 P. H. S., 3 B., 5 P. H. S., etc., all around.

8th row: Cr. 5 B., 3 P. H. S., 5 B., 3 P. H. S., etc., all around.

9th row: Cr. 7 B., 1 P. H. S., 7 B., 1 P. H. S., etc., all around.

10th row: Same as 8th row.

11th row: Same as 7th row.

12th row: Same as 6th row.

13th to 19th reverse order. Finish with loops of 30 B. catching same to every other St. of inverted cuff. Attach loops of 55 B. on to bottom of bag. Attach "Hiawatha" Drawstring cord.

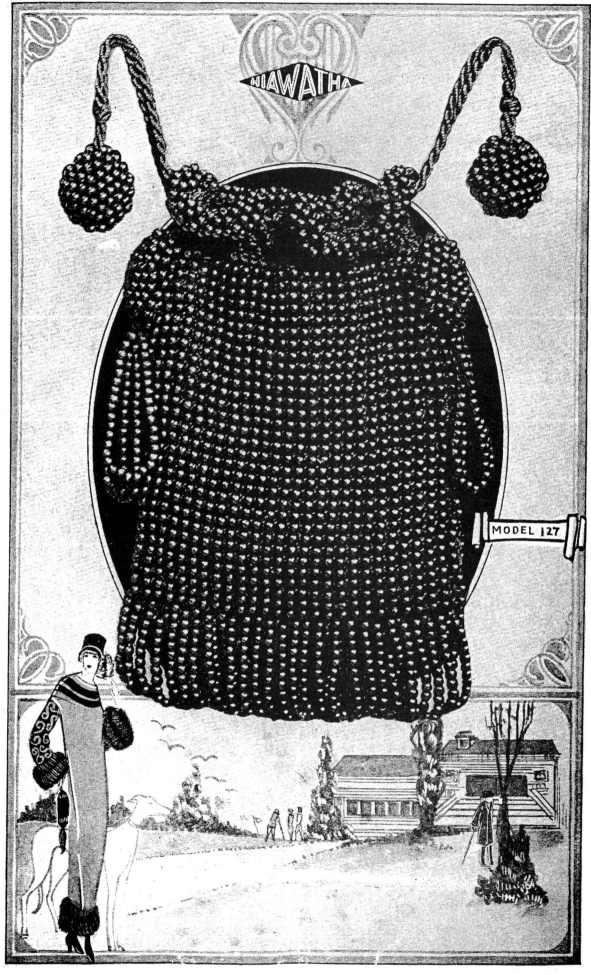

MODEL 127

"THE NEWPORT" No. 127

Materials: 3 Bunches "Hiawatha" "Ebonoid" Beads No. 3222.
1 Spool sweater silk. 2 "Hiawatha" steel knitting pins No. 10.
1 "Hiawatha" steel crochet hook No. 4.

With Hiawatha "Ebonoid" beads, very pretty effects can be obtained by contrasting colors of beads and silk.

Size of Bag: Width 6 inches—length 7 inches.

Cast on 28 St. on knitting pin, K. 1 row Pl. (without B.).

K. 31 rows with 1 B. in each St., always coming back with a row of Pl. on inside of bag.

On next row K. 1 Pl. slide 18 B. to form a loop. K. 1 Pl., etc., continue making loop fringes in this manner until end of line.

This completes one-half of the bag. Make the other half in the same manner, casting off stitches when finished. Sew bag up on sides.

Top of Bag: With crochet hook fasten silk at seam. Chain 4 and double Cr. into next St. Chain 1 and double Cr. in 2nd space. Continue in this way, making open meshes all around bag, until four rows are finished.

On the next row single Cr. 1 St. with a B. in each St. all around bag. Make 3 rows in this manner, then break thread and sew ends. Insert cord on top of bag through meshes.

Balls on end of cord: Chain 3 and join 2 St. with a B. in each St. Continue in this manner until there are 6 St. around. Start to increase work just enough to keep it cup shaped. After required size is reached (1½ inch diameter) decrease in the same manner as increased. Stuff with cotton.

Insert cord and sew firmly in opening of ball.

Cr. the disks on side of bag in the same manner as the balls on the ends of cord without decreasing and adding tassel of 5 loops of 30 beads each.

"THE KENILWORTH" No. 101

Illustrated on page 27

Materials: 11 Bunches Hiawatha Platinum Steel Beads, No. 9.
2 Spools Black or Navy Purse Twist.
1 "Hiawatha" bag chain No. 918.

Bold stripes of "Hiawatha" Platinum Steel Beads against a dark background lends a pleasing contrast.

Size of Bag: Width 5 inches. Length 7 inches.

Cr. 4 chains and join. Cr. alternately 1 P. H. S. and 1 B. until 9 B. are Cr.

3rd Line—Cr. alternately 1 P.H.S. and 2 B.

4th Line—1 P.H.S. and 3 B.

5th Line—1 P.H.S. and 4 B. The P.H.S. always being an increased st. Continue in this manner crocheting one additional B. to each group of the succeeding lines, until there are groups of 15 B. and 1 P.H.S.

From 16th Line, begin to use 2 B. less on each succeeding line, also inserting the zigzag design, as indicated on Chart A.

Continue in this fashion until bag measures 5½ inches.

Crochet 1¾ inches of P.H.S. and disconnect thread.

Inverted Cuff: Reverse work and connect thread. Cr. 2 chains, catching 2 B. on last chain, and Cr. on to border into third stitch. Make 4 lines of this. Make 1 line P.H.S. all around after which make diamonds as indicated on chart B. Then make 4 lines of 2 chains, etc., as above and end with loops of 32 beads each. Make Tassel—Attach Cord.

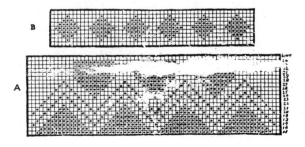

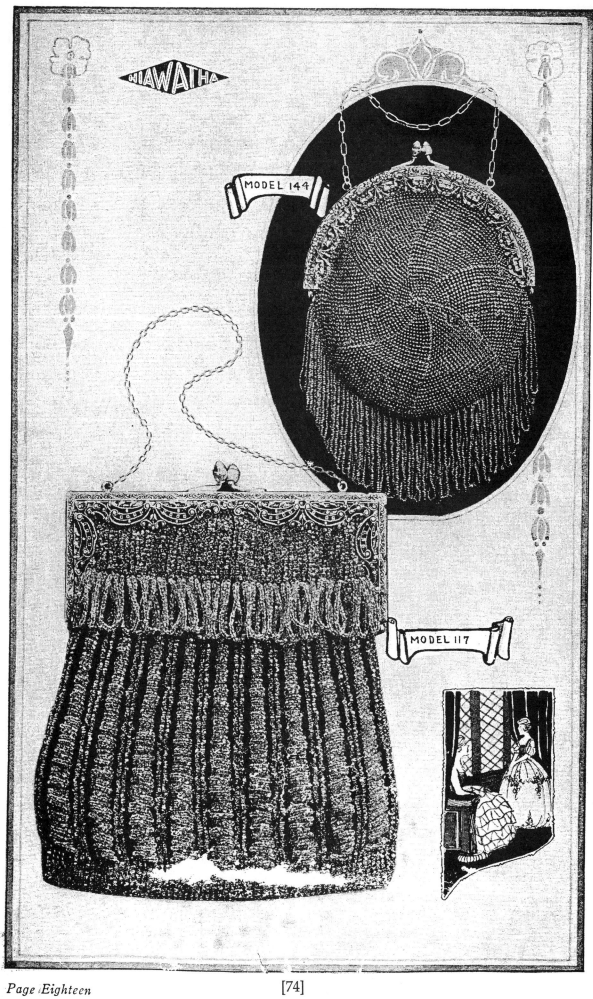

HIAWATHA

MODEL 144

MODEL 117

"THE RIALTO"
Model No. 144

Materials: 18 bunch round or cut steel beads size 8, 9 or 10.
2 Spools Purse Twist.
1 "Hiawatha" steel crochet hook No. 9.
1 "Hiawatha" bag frame No. 5959.

Model featured made with round steel beads, combined with grey purse twist.

Size of bag: Diameter 5 inches.
Chain 6 and join to form a ring.
Fill in with 12 H. St.
Crochet: 2 H. St. with B., 1 Pl., 2 H. St. with B., 1 Pl.
2 H. St. with B., 1 Pl., 2 H. St. with B., 1 Pl.
2 H. St. with B., 1 Pl., 2 H. St. with B., 1 Pl.

On the next row crochet 3 H. St. with B. and 1 Pl. until end of row. Continue in this manner always increasing 1 B. in every section until 35 B. are in each section. This completes one side of bag.
Crochet the other side in exactly the same manner.
Fringe: Crochet a fringe, half around, on one side of bag, four inches turned up, making a two inch fringe.
Mounting: Line with silk and attach frame.

"THE SOPHOMORE"
Model No. 117

Materials: 24 Bchs. "Hiawatha" cut beads 9/0.
2 Spools Purse Twist.
1 Pair "Hiawatha" Knitting Pins No. 18.
1 Pair "Hiawatha" Knitting Pin Protectors.
1 "Hiawatha" Filigree Frame No. 5884/6.

Graduated columns and stripes of single beads, brings forth the excellence of the Crystal Gems No. 21/9 on a background of jade green Purse Twist.

Size of bag: Width 6 inches. Length 7 inches.
Cast on 69 St. K. 3 ridges Pl. (without beads). K. 12 ridges with 1 B. in each St., always coming back with a line of Pl. (no beads) on inside of bag.
Make 1 row of loops of 34 B. each with a Pl. St. between each loop.
K. 1 ridge Pl.
18th ridge: K. 2 Pl. * 2 B. 2 Pl. Slide 2 B. K. 2 Pl. *. Repeat from * to * till end of line. When coming back on inside of bag to complete ridge K. as follows: 6 Pl. Slide 2 B. 6 Pl. Slide 2 B., etc., etc., till end of line.
Note: When knitting back on inside of bag always knit 6 Pl. before sliding beads.
The following 63 ridges are made in exactly the same manner with the exception of the slides which are made as follows:

12 ridges—slide 2 beads	9 ridges—slide 6 beads
11 ridges—slide 3 beads	7 ridges—slide 7 beads
10 ridges—slide 4 beads	7 ridges—slide 8 beads
10 ridges—slide 5 beads	

Bottom Band: K. 6 Pl. Cast on 2 St. K. 6 Pl. Cast on 2 St., etc., until end of row. Then K. 20 lines with a single B. in each St., always coming back with a row of Pl (no beads) on inside of bag.
Next row: K. 6 Pl., cast off 2 St. St., etc., until end of row.
Continue balance of bag by reversing the order. Sew up sides.
Line bag with piece of silk and attach frame.

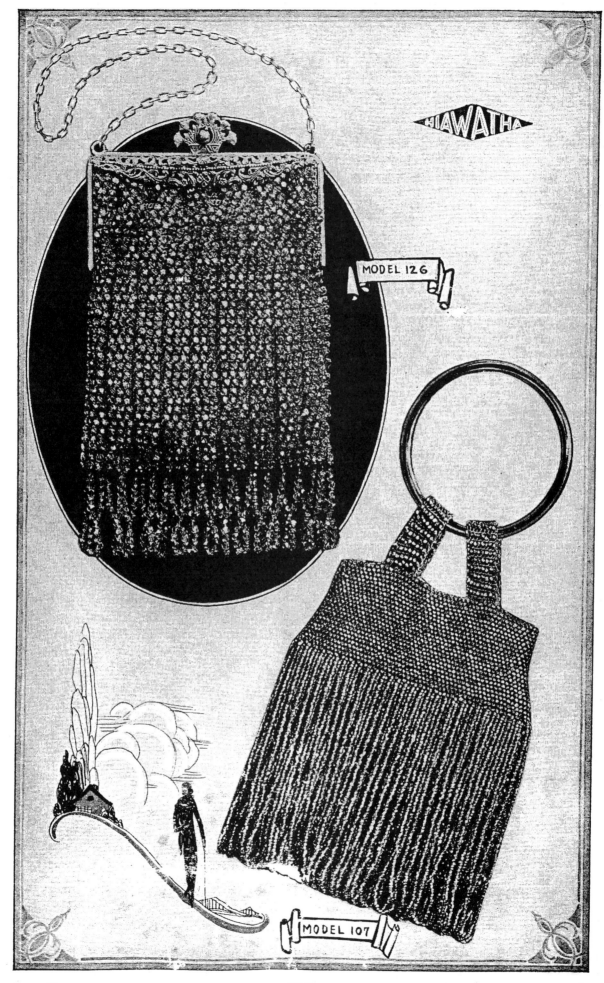

MODEL 126

MODEL 107

"THE THAMES" No. 126

Materials: 4 Bchs. "Hiawatha" crystallized gems 2648 or "Silver Glo Gems" No. 3117.
2 spools purse twist.
1 Hiawatha Crochet Hook No. 9.
1 Hiawatha Filigree Frame No. 5859.

This model looks well with any blended or contrasting color of beads and silk.

Size of bag: Width 4½ inches—length 6 inches.

Bottom of bag: Ch. 54, Cr. on each side of Ch. 1 row of Pl. St. without beads *. On next row Cr. 3 B. with St. between each bead—then 3 Pl. St. *. Repeat from * to * 8 times more, making 9 columns across the bag. Cr. 1 row of Pl. St., Cr. 22 rows in this manner, always with 1 line of Pl. St. between each row of B., Cr. 23rd row the same as preceding rows, leaving an opening on sides for frame. Cr. 13 rows in this manner.
Finish off with 2 rows of Pl. St.

Fringe: Fasten silk to end of bag and string 15 beads and go back through the 7th B. from the top. String 6 more B. and fasten to bag. Repeat 15 times. Line with silk and attach frame.

"THE FRENCH ENVELOPE" No. 146

Illustrated on page 26

Materials: 6 Bunches Star Brand cut steel beads size 8 or 9.
4 Bunches colored metal beads size 8.
1 Spool each of navy and grey purse twist.
6 Dozen each of red and blue jewels number 2731 or 3118.
1 "Hiawatha" filigree envelope rod number 5936.

The contrasting colors of the silk, beads and jewels gives this model an impressive appearance. This bag also makes up very nicely with copen, jade, gold or blue metal beads, combined with the cut steel beads.

Size of Bag: Width 5½ inches. Length 3½ inches.

Size of Flap: Width 5½ inches. Length 1¼ inches.

String 2 bunches of red beads on grey silk and chain 76 St., Cr. on each side of Ch. 1 row of H. St. (no beads).

3rd row: Cr. with 1 red B. in each st. all around.
*4th row: Cr. 7b. 1 pl. 7 b. 1 pl. etc. all around.
5th row: Cr. 5 b. 3 pl. 5 b. 3 pl. etc. all around.
6th row: Cr. 3 b. 5 pl. 3 b. 5 pl. etc. all around.
7th row: Cr. 1 b. 7 pl. 1 b. 7 pl. etc. all around.
8th row: Cr. 3 b. 5 pl. 3 b. 5 pl. etc. all around.
9th row: Cr. 5 b. 3 pl. 5 b. 3 pl. etc. all around.
10th row: Cr. 7 b. 1 pl. 7 b. 1 pl. etc. all around.
11th row: Cr. with 1 b. in each st. all around then break thread. *
Repeat from * to * using navy purse twist and steel beads.
Repeat from * to * using grey purse twist and red beads.
Repeat from * to * using navy purse twist and steel beads.
Repeat from * to * using grey purse twist and red beads.
Repeat from * to * using navy purse twist and steel beads.

Flap: Cr. on one-half the bag only, in the same manner repeating from * to * using grey purse twist and red beads.

Note: To keep flap straight, crochet 20 chain stitches at the end of each line.

Repeat from * to * using navy purse twist and steel beads.
Finish flap with loop fringes of 35 b. each.
Then cut chain stitches and finish off with buttonhole stitch on each side to prevent ripping.

Fringe on bottom of bag is made, by sewing alternately 1 loop of steel beads and 1 loop of red beads   loop being 1 inch long.
Slip flap through envelope rod.
Sew blue jewels on the grey silk diamonds and red jewels on the blue silk diamonds. Each jewel to be sewn individually.

Line bag with piece of silk and sew snap fastener in centre of bag.

MODEL 139

MODEL 112

HIAWATHA

"THE PERLENE" No. 139 *Illustrated on page 22*

Materials: 10 Bchs. "Hiawatha" PERLENE Beads No. 400
1 Spool Purse Twist to match.
1 "Hiawatha" Steel Crochet Hook No. 9.
½ Gross Jewels No. 2530/15.
1 "Hiawatha" Frame No. 5939.

Original model illustrated made with white "Perlene" Beads No. 400/1 and white purse twist.

Size of bag: Width 3 inches—length 4½ inches.

Chain 4 inches to start. Cr. on both sides of chain with whole St. for 8 rows. On the next row Cr. 1 B. with 1 H. St. and a 4 inch loop

Continued on page 25

"THE PIROUETTE" No. 112 *Illustrated on page 22*

Materials: 8 Bchs. "Hiawatha" Cut Beads 9/0.
1 Spool Purse Twist.
1 "Hiawatha" Steel Crochet Hook No. 10.
1 "Hiawatha" Filigree Frame No. 5680.

Sunset beads No. 1525/32 with purse twist to match makes a dainty dance or party bag.

Size of bag: Width 2½ inches—length 4½ inches.

Ch. 6 and join. Cr. in each Ch. 2 loops (4 inches long) for the tassel. Then Cr. 24 whole St.

Continue crocheting with whole St. increasing in each row for 3 rows to keep the work flat.

Next row Cr. 1 H. St. with 1 B. and 1 H. St. with 30 B. forming a loop. Repeat all around bag.

Then Cr. 3 rows of whole St. * Cr. 1 row of loops as before (1 H. St. with 1 B. and 1 H. St. with 30 B. forming a loop.) * Cr. 3 more rows of whole St. then repeat from * to *. Continue by Cr. 2 chains and 1 B. with 1 H. St. for 13 rows. ** Cr. 3 rows of whole St. across half of the bag decreasing at each end to fit the frame. ** Then Cr. 1 row of loops as described from * to *, making 21 loops. Cr. 3 rows of whole St. and 1 row of 17 loops and then 3 rows of whole St. finishing one side of bag. For the other half of the bag repeat from ** to **.

Line with silk and attach frame.

Handle: Ch. 7 to start. Cr. 1 row of H. St. plain and 1 row of H. St. with B. and back 1 row Pl., etc., etc., until handle measures 8 inches. Line handle with piece of silk and attach to top of frame.

"THE SUNSHOWER" No. 107 *Illustrated on page 20*

Materials: 21 Bchs. "Hiawatha" Cut Beads 9/0.
1 Pair "Hiawatha" Rings No. 1903 or 3137.
2 Spools Purse Twist.
1 "Hiawatha" Steel Crochet Hook No. 9.

Bronze transparent-irridescent beads No. 2569/1 with French Blue Purse Twist makes an ideal combination for this model.

Size of bag: Width 5 inches—length 5¼ inches.

Start with 65 chain St. or about 5 inches long. Cr. on both sides of chain 1 row of P. H. S. On the next row Cr. alternately 1 P. H. S. with 1 B. and 1 H. St. plain. Cr. on top of Pl. St. 1 B. and on top of B. 1 Pl. St. Continue in this manner, always alternating the Pl. St. and the B. Work 48 rows, then make 1 row of Pl. St., decreasing 2 St. at each end.

Long Loops: Cr. 1 St. with 1 B. and the next St. with a 9 inch loop. Repeat all around bag.

Then Cr. 24 rows of solid B. dec. in the 2 B. on every 3rd row.

Straps for Handle: Ch. 7 to start. Cr. 1 line Pl., then 1 line with B., 1 line Pl., etc., until strap measures 3 inches. Make 4 straps and attach 2 on each side of bag and insert rings as illustrated.

Line bag with silk.

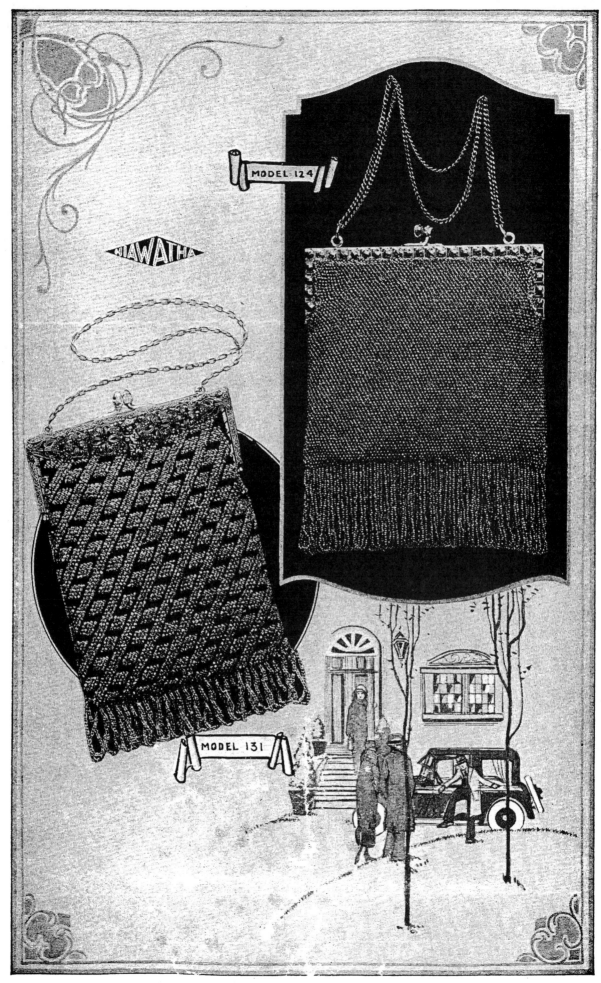

HIAWATHA

MODEL 124

MODEL 131

"THE CHANTILLY" No. 124

Materials: 15 Bchs "Star Brand" cut steel beads size 8-9 or 10.
2 spools grey spurse twist.
1 "Hiawatha" steel crochet Hook No. 9.
1 "Hiawatha" French steel frame No. 4089/14.

This bag made with cut steel beads and mounted on a steel bag frame combines simplicity of design with smart appearance.

Size of Bag: Width 5½ inches—lenth 5 inches.

Bottom of Bag: Cr. about 60 ch. st. or 5½ inches long. Cr. on both sides of Ch. 1 Row of P. H. S. On next row cr. H. St. with B. in each St. Continue in this manner till bag measures 3½ inches. Begin opening for bag frame). Cr. next row same as preceding row decreasing 3 St. on each side, Cr. 10 ch. St. without B. on each side. Repeat last line till bag measures 5 inches. Sew on loop fringe 1½ inches long close together. Insert lining.

Mount frame by cutting the ch. st. and finishing off with button hole st. to prevent ripping.

"THE COUNTRY CLUB" No. 131

Materials: 17 Bchs. "Hiawatha" cut Beads 9/0.
2 spools Purse Twist.
1 "Hiawatha" Steel Crochet Hook No. 9.
1 "Hiawatha" Filigree Frame No. 5876/5.

A charming effect can be produced by contrasting color of beads and silk.

Size of Bag: Width 5 inches. Length 6 inches.

Chain 60. Cr. on each side of Ch. as follows:

1st row: * 4 H. St. with 1 B. in each St. 1 P. H. S., 3 B., 1 P. H. S., * Repeat from * to * 13 times around the bag.

2nd row: Cr. over the 1st B. in the previous row 1 P. H. S., then 4 B., 1 P. H. S., 3 B., 1 P. H. S., etc., all around the bag.

Continue in this manner crocheting 1 P. H. S. above the 1st B. in the previous row, thus getting the oblique design as illustrated.

On the 58th to 82nd rows, Cr. 3 Pl. St. and 12 chains at each end of bag for opening of frame.

Fringe: Cr. 1 row of loops across bottom of bag, making each loop 3 inches doubled up.

Lining and Mounting: Line bag with piece of silk, then cut open chain stitches at each side of bag and attach frame.

DESIGN USED THROUGHOUT THE BAG

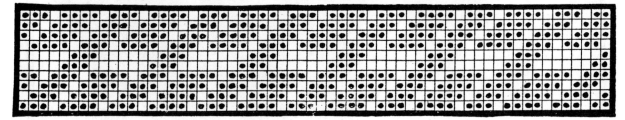

● BEADS   □ PLAIN HALF STITCHES

MODEL No. 139 *Continued from page 23*

with the next H. St. Repeat all around bag. Continue crocheting the next 8 rows with whole St. Then Cr. 1 B. with 1 H. St. and a 4 inch loop with the next H. St.

* On the next row Cr. half the bag, back and forth with whole St. plain and 1 row of H. St. with B. and back 1 row plain, etc., etc., decreasing at each end to fit the frame. Crochet 8 rows in this manner *. Crochet the other half of bag as from * to *.

Sew jewels evenly in spaces between the rows of beads on top.

Line with piece of silk and attach frame.

Handle: Chain 7 to start. Cr. 1 row H. St. plain and 1 row H. St. with B. and back 1 row plain, etc., etc., until handle measures 8 inches.

Line handle with piece of silk and attach to top of frame.

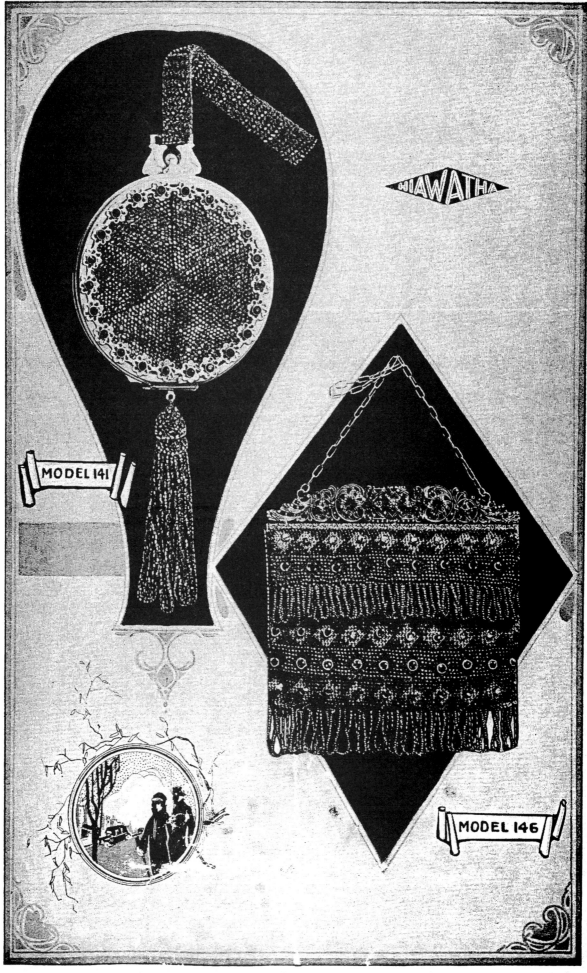

HIAWATHA

MODEL 141

MODEL 146

MODEL No. 141 *Described on Page 7*
MODEL No. 146 *Described on Page 21*

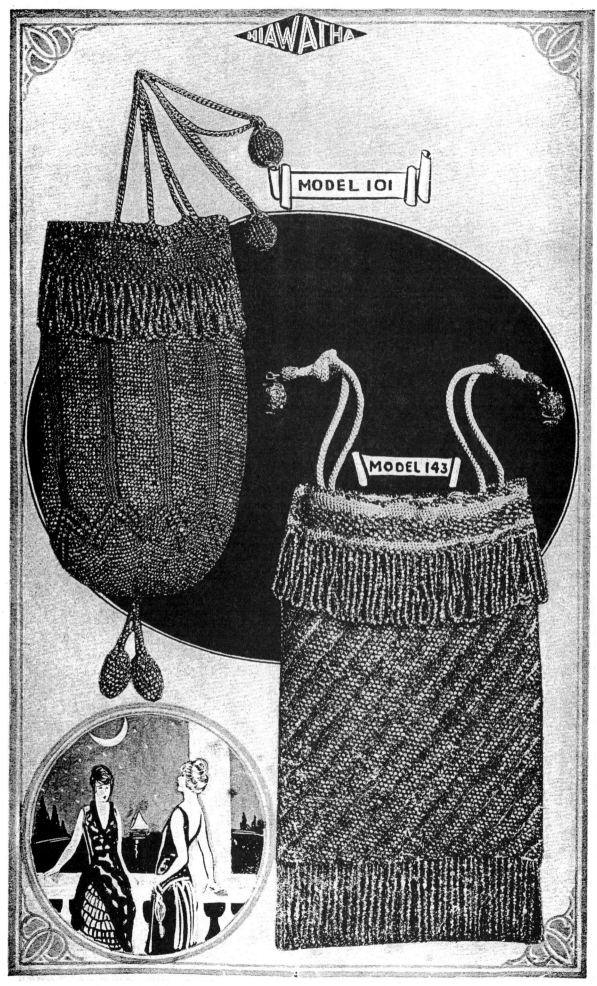

MODEL No. 101 *Described on Page 17*   MODEL No. 143 *Described on Page 15*   *Page Twenty-Seven*

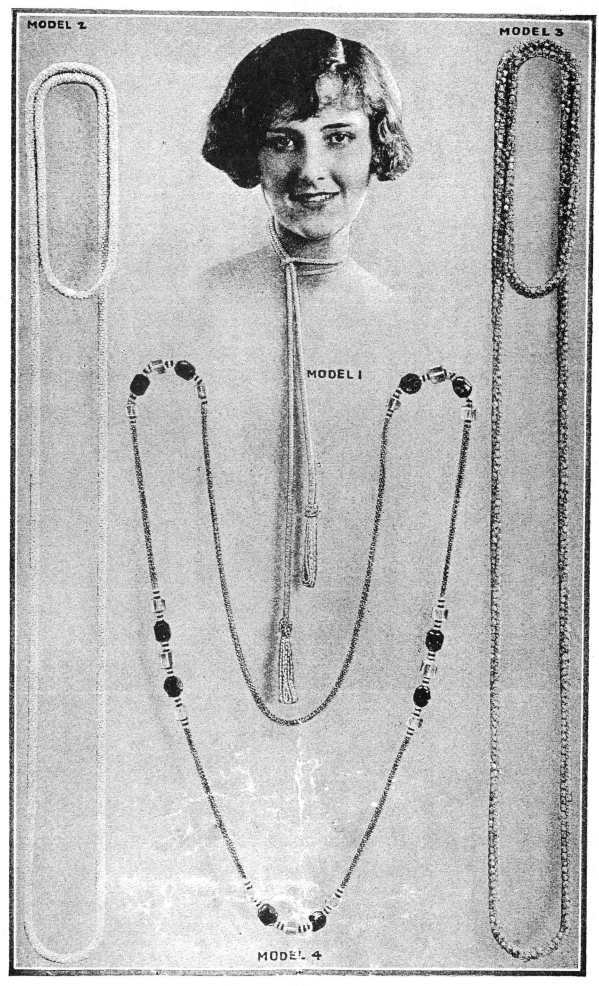

MODEL 2

MODEL 3

MODEL I

MODEL 4

"THE HIAWATHA CHAIN" No. 1

Materials: 5 Bchs. "Hiawatha" Brilliant Lustre Beads No.
1525 or 2718, or "Hiawatha" Bead Reel No. 2795
(See note below.)
1 "Hiawatha Crochet Hook No. 10.
50 yards button hole twist.
2 Pc. round or square Venetian Beads.

Allow 12 inches of silk and Ch. 5. Put hook in chain nearest to hook *. Push up a bead single crochet or (slip stitch) *. Put hook into the next chain and repeat from * to *. Repeat until there are 4 beads in a row, then join by putting hook under the thread the first bead is on. Push up another bead single crochet or (slip stitch). This makes five beads in each row.

Continue this way by going behind each bead, catching the thread the bead is on, crocheting around and around until the chain measures required length or about 54 inches.

Tassels: Put a Venetian bead on each end and attach tassel 8 strands, 3 inches long doubled up.

Note: With a "Hiawatha" bead reel no button hole twist or stringing is required. Beads come all strung, ready to be crocheted.

THE PERLENE ENDLESS CHAIN No. 2

Materials: 5 Bchs. "Perlene" beads No. 400.
50 yards. button hole twist.
1 "Hiawatha" Crochet Hook No. 10.

The crocheting on this chain is done exactly the same as No. 1 except there are six beads in a row instead of five and crocheting the ends together instead of putting tassels on.

THE WATER LILY CHAIN No. 3

Materials: 2 Bchs. "Hiawatha" crystalized gems 2648.
1 Hiawatha crochet hook No. 10.
50 Yds. buttonhole twist or tatting thread.

The crocheting on this chain is done exactly the same as No. 1 except that there are 3 beads in a row instead of 6.

THE "CUBIST" WOVEN CHAIN No. 4

Materials: 2 Spools button hole twist.
2 Bchs. No. 9 or 10 cut or round steel beads.
2 "Hiawatha" beading needles.
Large fancy or Venetian and rondelles about 2
dozen or enough to complete the group design.

Instructions: Thread 2 needles, one at each end of a four yard piece of silk thread. **On needle No. 1 string the large glass beads, according to the design desired. Then put needle No. 2 through the same beads.

String the steel beads on needle No. 1 until the desired length is reached, this will be the spacing between the groups of fancy beads. Then with needle No. 2 pick up one steel bead and go through second bead, picking up one more and going through fourth bead, etc., etc. Continue in this manner always skipping one bead, and going through the following beads.**

Repeat from ** to ** until there are five sections of large fancy beads.

String 12 inches of steel beads, weaving these as explained, and connecting them at the starting point, by going through the first three large beads.

After chain is completed, thread another needle and starting at the beginning pass the needle through the first design. Pass the needle through the first steel bead on the outside row. Pick up a steel bead and pass the needle through the second steel bead on the outside row. Continue in this manner until the whole chain is completed.

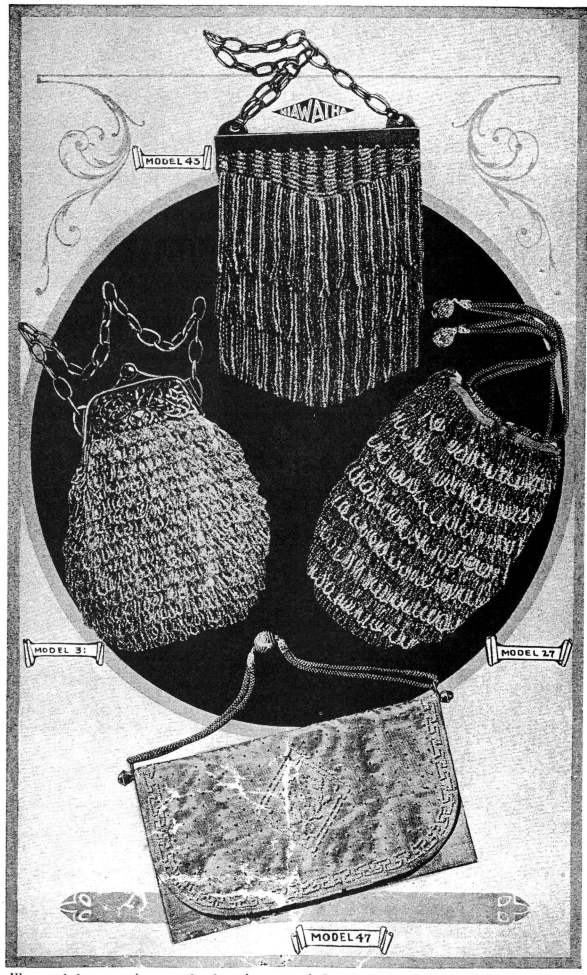

MODEL 43

MODEL 3:

MODEL 27

MODEL 47

Illustrated above are a few up-to-date bags th... *made by ordinary sewing with Hiawatha stamped*
patterns. Complete instructions con... pattern, no knitting nor crocheting necessary.

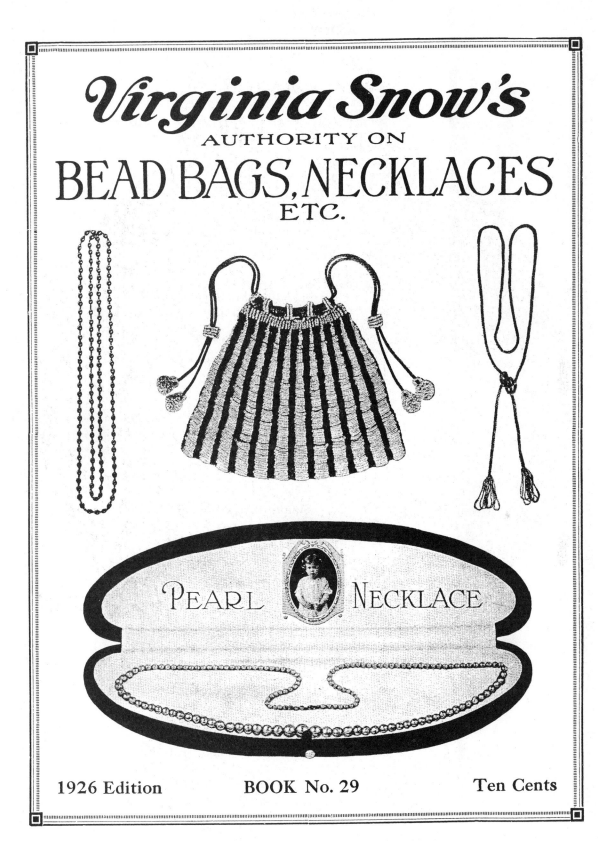

Virginia Snow's
AUTHORITY ON
BEAD BAGS, NECKLACES
ETC.

PEARL NECKLACE

1926 Edition   BOOK No. 29   Ten Cents

EXAMPLES OF MODERN HANDICRAFT. SO SIMPLE EVERY LADY MAY BEAUTIFY THE BOUDOIR, VANITY TABLE, TEA TABLE, LIBRARY, ETC.

Simple Instructions for Making
THE "HILCRAFT" SHADE
Lesson by Virginia Snow

Beads required: Crystal Iridescent. 10 strings of size 2/0; 11 strings of size 0; 7 strings of size 2. A string is 50 beads. Also 6 Crystal Pendants, size 18.

You will need 1/6 yard of China Silk 36 or 40 inches wide; 1 yard of silver braid; 1 wire frame, 6½ inches in diameter at the base, 3 inches at top, 4 inches high, and one spool of Lamp Shade Twist, Art 1183.

Bind the entire frame with white seam binding. Pin one long side to base of frame on the inside and overcast. Draw other long end up tightly, arranging to have the fullness well distributed. Overcast to top wire. Draw opposite ends of plaits down to wire at base of frame, drawing it tightly and spacing the plaits an equal distance apart, so the plaits are straight on the shade.

Overcast top and bottom. Sew to base of shade and cover stitches with a strip of silver braid. The beads around the shade and for fringe are looped around the shade. There are 5 loops on each side and about 28 beads for each loop of the fringe.

There are 3 loops in the fringe. Place a large pendulum bead at each intersection of the fringe.

THE HILCRAFT SHADE

LAMP SHADE TWIST is an enameled strong thread for stringing beads and sewing over wire lamp shade frames or for millinery purposes. **50 yards to spool. All staple colors. Per spool...................5c**

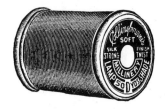

Simple Instructions for Making
THE "CARPENTER CRYSTAL" SHADE
Lesson by Virginia Snow

Beads required: Crystal Iridescent. 16 strings of size 2/0; 15 strings of size 0; 16 strings of size 2. A string is 50 beads. Also 30 Crystal Slides, size 12, and 30 Crystal Pendants, size 18.

You will need 1 spool of Lamp Shade Twist, Art 1183; 1 yard of silver braid; 1 wire frame, 6½ inches in diameter at the base, 3 inches at top, 4 inches high. Bind the entire frame with white seam binding. String 28 graduated beads on a double thread as follows: 10 small at top, 8 medium in center, 10 large at bottom, and tie to the frame at top and bottom. Repeat until entire frame is covered.

Fringe: Two shapes of pendulum beads are used with the medium size bead at the top and the larger size at the bottom of each pendulum. Group them on shade as in illustration. Bind the top and bottom of shade with silver braid.

THE CARPENTER CRYSTAL SHADE

[88]

1   2   3   4

STYLISH AND POPULAR BEAD NECKLACES

Styles 1, 2 and 3 represent the simple art of stringing beads in any color combination or size to suite the gown or occasion, such as street wear or the ballroom.

DIRECTIONS FOR MAKING STYLE 4 BEAD CHAIN

Materials: 5 bunches beads, 40 yards of Purse Twist.

Directions: String 4 bunches on the Purse Twist. Chain 5, then put a bead in each chain stitch and join. Crochet around and around with a single crochet and put a bead in each stitch. Continue crocheting until the chain is 54 inches long. Attach a tassel 3 inches long of 5 double strands of beads.

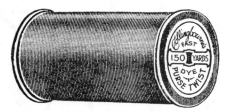

UNBREAKABLE
"It's the Quality"

WATER-PROOF
"It's the Quality"

Purse Twist—150 Yard Spool.

This Bead Cord or Purse Twist has been specially processed to add strength and durability and is BEST for stringing and sewing all kinds of beads, is smooth and water-proof, for all necklaces, bags, purses and dress trimmings.

DIRECTIONS FOR MAKING PEARL NECKLACE (Shown Above)

Materials: 24 bunches beads, 40 yards of Purse Twist.

Directions: String 16 bunches on the Purse Twist. Chain 5, then put a bead in each chain stitch and join. Crochet around and around with a single crochet and put a bead in each stitch. Continue crocheting until the chain is 54 inches long. Attach a tassel 3 inches long of 4 double strands of beads.

THE CORRECT METHOD TO STRING A BEAD NECKLACE

First take desired length of cord, 36 inches or more, from the 150 yard spool, then make double knot at one end and thread other end into thread beads are on, or use No. 15-B fine needle and string 4 beads, drawing the cord through one eye of the clasp and drawing it back through the four beads. String the balance of the Necklace and finish by drawing Collingbourne's bead cord through the other eye of the clasp, then bring the cord back through four beads, make a double knot and draw cord through a few more beads.

THE CORRECT METHOD TO STRING BEADS FOR DRESS TRIMMINGS, ETC.

Start the cord in fabric, using desirable needle length with No. 15-B needle, then thread bead on cord singly or in groups, according to pattern, using the common back stitch, fastening beads to pattern on fabric.

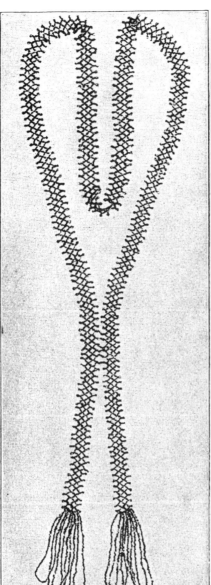

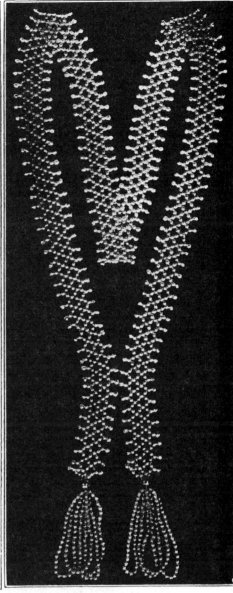

Pearl Chain No. 3   Flat Bead Chain No. 5   Flat Bead Chain No. 6

Instructions For Making Novelty Pearl Chain No. 3

Materials: 48 large Pearls No. 38, 12 small Pearls, No. 31, 4 bunches Seed Beads (any color), 1 spool Purse Twist.

Directions: Thread fine bead needle with Purse Twist. Have thread about 46 in. long. Take a large Pearl No. 38. String 10 seed Beads. String one large Pearl No. 38, then 10 seed Beads. Continue until you have 48 Pearls strung. Start with a new thread. Go thru the large Pearl already strung. String 10 seed beads, then go thru large Pearl (already strung). Continue until end of string thru 48th Pearl. Start with a new thread, and do as above, stringing 10 seed beads, then running needle thru Pearl bead. When completed, you should have **4 strings of the 10 seed Beads, with one large Pearl No. 38 between every 10th bead.** Ends may be finished with a tassel.

Instructions For Making Novelty Flat Bead Chains No. 5 and No. 6

Materials: For No. 5 Bead Chain, 5 bunches Seed Beads (any color) and one Spool Purse Twist.

Materials: For No. 6 Bead Chain, 23 Strings Pearl Beads No. 31 and one Spool Purse Twist.

Directions: Thread fine bead needle with Twist—about 15 in. thread. String 7 beads. Go back thru 2nd bead from end. String 3 beads. Go into 2nd bead from end of the 7 beads. String 3 beads. Go back thru 2nd bead of the 3 just strung. TURN CHAIN OVER. String 3 beads. Go into 4th bead from end. String 3 beads. Go thru 2nd bead of the 3 just strung. TURN CHAIN OVER. String 3 beads. Go into 4th bead from end. String 3 beads. Go thru 2nd bead of the 3 just strung. TURN CHAIN OVER. Proceed with above until chain is desired length. ALWAYS put on 3 beads. REMEMBER: Go thru 2nd, 4th and 2nd bead. TURN. When thread gets near end, work in and out thru beads, so as to fasten end. Then work a **new** thread in and out thru beads so as to fasten.

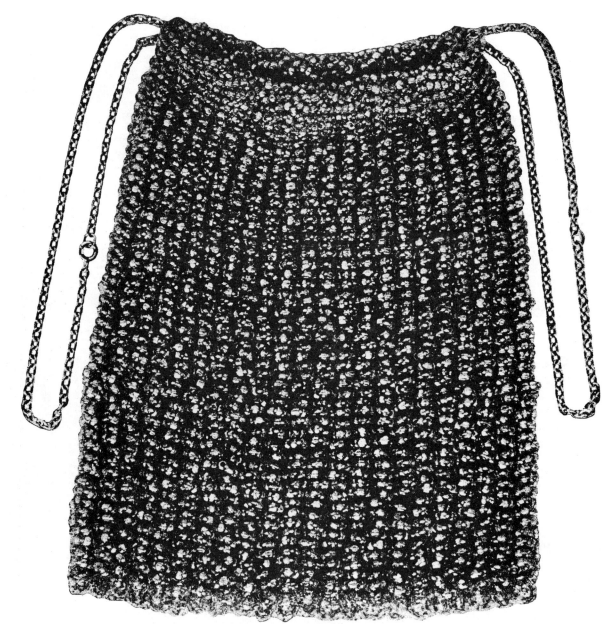

Canton Bag No. 1
A CHARMING BEAD BAG IN VOGUE

Materials required: 1 spool Purse Twist. 5 bunches of beads, 1 pair steel knitting needles.

Directions: Cast on 46 sts., hold the two needles together and cast sts. on this, then pull out one needle. On coming back, slip a bead after each st. Knit next row plain. Continue beading on one side till there are 7 rows of beads.

There are 1 st. and 1 bead on either edge the full length of bag. There are 2 sts. between the panels of beads.

If the bag is to be mounted on a frame, leave 1 bead off on the edges for the first 15 ridges to sew into frame. Remembering 1 st. on edges and 2 between panels of beads, slip beads according to following:

RIDGES	BEADS
4	1-2-2-2, etc., and 1 st. on end
5	1-3-3-3, etc., and 1 st. on end
7	1-4-4-4, etc., and 1 st. on end
8	1-5-5-5, etc., and 1 st. on end
9	1-6-6-6, etc., and 1 st. on end
20	1-7-7-7, etc., and 1 st. on end

53 Ridges—One-half of bag.

Always increase or decrease width of bag by 4 sts. One row is knitted plain, the other with beads the entire length of bag.

Sides either sewed or crocheted together.

Amateur Model No. 3

THE YOUNG LADY AMATEUR MAY MAKE THIS

Simply purchase any stamped bag pattern on fabric. String the same number of beads on bead **cord** for each loop and sew the cord into fabric, following design of pattern carefully. Blend any combination of colors in beads to suit your ideal.

Copleigh Bag No. 4

BLACK PURSE TWIST AND CRYSTAL BEADS

Materials required: 2 spools Purse Twist, 10 bunches of beads, 1 pair steel knitting needles.

Directions: String 2 bunches. Cast on 52 stitches. Knit off 2 stitches. Then knit one bead in every stitch for four rows on either side. Then knit off 2 stitches —slip one bead in. Then knit 4 stitches, then one bead—four stitches till you have 3 rows on either side. Then knit off 2 stitches and slip 2 beads— four stitches two beads—for four rows on either side. Then cast off 2 stitches. Slip three beads—

four stitches. Three beads for six rows of either side. Knit off 2 stitches—slip four beads. Four stitches for 8 rows.

Slip 5 beads for 10 rows.
Slip 6 beads for 12 rows.
Slip 7 beads for 22 rows.

This makes one-half of the bag. Continue and make 22 rows more of seven beads—12 rows of 6 beads, etc.

[94]

A B C
BAG

THE A B C BAG

Materials: 1 spool Purse Twist, navy; 8 bunches blue iridescent beads, and No. 11 crochet hook.

String only 2 bunches of beads on a spool of Purse Twist at one time. String rest of beads as needed.

Ch. 8, join to form a ring.

8 d. c. into ch.

(1 d. c. with bead, 1 d. c. without in first stitch, repeat 7 times.)

(1 d. c. with bead in each of 2 stitches, 1 d. c. without bead in second stitch, repeat 7 times.)

(1 d. c. with bead in each of three stitches, 1 d. c. without bead in third stitch, repeat 7 times.)

Continue until there are 14 beads in each section. Then make 6 rows without widening, with a bead in each stitch. Make 3 rows using s. c. instead of d. c. with a bead in each stitch. See that there are 126 stitches in the last row made. Then make s. c. without bead in each of three stitches and s. c. with bead in each of three stitches all around bag. *Next Row*—To start, make 2 stitches without beads and continue making 3 stitches with beads, 3 stitches without beads and 3 stitches with beads all around bag. *Next Row*—To start, make 1 stitch without bead and continue making 3 stitches with beads, 3 stitches without beads and 3 stitches with beads all around bag. *Next Row*—Make 2 stitches without beads, 3 stitches with beads and so on, decreasing in same manner as increased. This will add 5 more rows.

Then make 3 more rows of s. c. with a bead in each stitch.

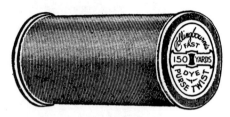

Purse Twist

Make 7 rows of d. c. with a bead in each stitch.

Chain 4, fasten in 3rd stitch, chain 4 and fasten in 6th stitch and continue around bag. Slip-stitch to center of next chain and chain 4 fastening into center of next chain of row below and continue making 9 rows of chains.

For cuff, turn work and crochet opposite way. Push on 2 beads and chain 4, fasten in center of chain 4 of row before. Continue round and round, making 6 rows.

Straighten edge of cuff by chain 3 fastened into center of each chain of row below. Make 1 row of s. c. without beads and 4 rows of s. c. with beads. For bead fringe, put 40 beads in each loop and crochet into every other stitch.

Beading—Make 2 d. c. chain 4 and 2 d. c. around top of bag. Finish with shell stitch edge.

Cord—Take 3 thicknesses of thread and crochet two chains 18 inches long and run through top of bag for draw strings.

Make tassel of 10 loops of 80 beads each and fasten to bottom of bag. Line bag with silk or sateen to finish.

MISER BAG

Materials required: 2 spools Purse Twist, 4 bunches of beads, crochet hook No. 11.

Directions: String 2 bunches of No. 8 steel cut beads on gray Purse Twist. Chain 85 stitches. Work around chain for one row with double stitch. Work around again with double stitch for 8 rows. String 2 bunches of beads on dark blue Purse Twist. Attach blue to gray and work around with the blue twice with double crochet stitch and at the beginning of the third row make a loop of ten beads—put one of these loops in every fifth stitch until you have seventeen loops. Then work around plain double crochet for one row. Then another row of loops and so on until you have eight rows of loops. Attach gray thread and repeat the eight rows of plain double crochet with a bead in each stitch. Attach blue thread and work around with a triple stitch in every other stitch for eighteen rows. This is one-half of the bag. Put a fringe on one end of the bag. Draw the other together and put on a tassel.

DAINTY KNITTED BAG

Materials: 15 bunches of beads, 1 spool of Purse Twist, and 1 pair steel knitting needles, No. 19.

String 3 bunches of beads at a time. Cast on 63 stitches. Knit one row, slipping first stitch. Knit 3 stitches, slip 1 bead, and knit 3 more stitches. Repeat this across and back, (1 row) for 5 rows.

The sixth row slip 2 beads for 6 rows; 3 beads for 7 rows; 4 beads for 8 rows; 5 beads for 9 rows. This makes half the bag. Begin at this point and reverse the order. Knit one row plain and bind off. Sew up sides and line with satin. Finish with rings and cord.

COLLINGBOURNE'S, ART. C51 CORDONETT, SIZE 5, WHITE OR ECRU

Is the Correct Cord for Making Window Shade Cord and Tassels.

Directions: Over cardboard, 4 inches wide, wind thread about 100 times—cut threads at one end and wind a thread over what is now the center, tightly three times, leaving thread sufficiently long to pass through a needle, and sew to window shade afterwards.

About ½ an inch below this thread, wind over tassel another thread 10 times, tightly and evenly, which completes the top of the tassel; fasten this thread by passing it up and down in center of parts just wound.

Make chain about ¾ yard long—make simple knots in chain, about 2 inches apart—sew to bottom of wound part, making loops to the length of the tassel—this will give 4 loops of the chain.

Artificial Silk Crochet Twist For Lamp Shade Fringe

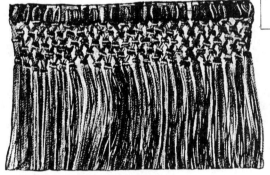

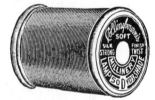

For sewing fabrics on wire frames use Lamp Shade Twist

LAMP SHADE FRINGE

Cut cardboard about 5 inches long. Wind one ball of Luxura and cut all the threads at one end. Take 6 strands and double same. Insert large crochet hook through shade from the under side near edge of frame and draw the double ends of the 6 threads from the upper side forming a loop of 6 threads on the under side. Through this loop draw the 12 ends and draw close to the end of the frame making a smooth knot.

Repeat the process all the way around the shade.

Repeat the process in as many rows of knots as the taste of the individual desires. However, 5 rows are considered sufficient.

After the fringe is completed, expose all the wrinkled parts of the fringe freely to the steam from the spout of a boiling tea kettle until all the wrinkles are smoothed out, and then allow same to dry.

PURE SILK

EXTRA STRONG AND SPECIALLY PROCESSED

COLLINGBOURNE'S

GOLD MEDAL Pure Silk Purse and Bead Twist, Art. 25

Made in the following colors.

800	White	885	Red
805	Black	894	Jade Green
817	Gold	934	Brown
837	Navy	968	Purple
838	Dk. Navy	984	Grey
843	Admiral Blue.		

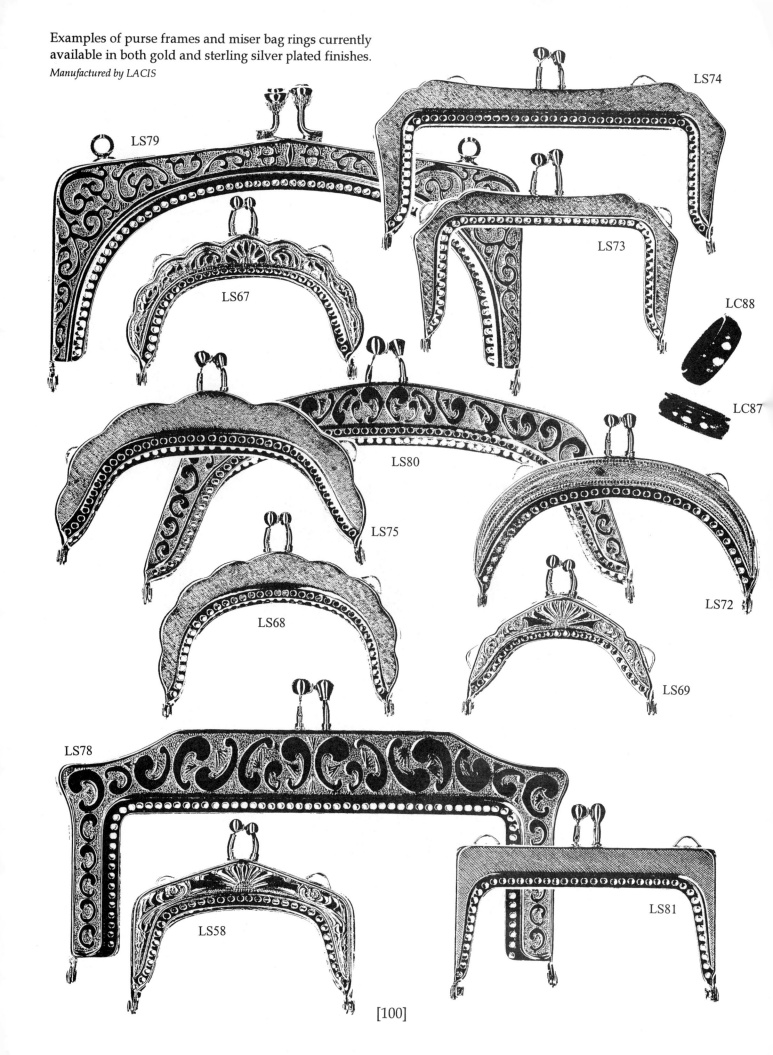

Examples of purse frames and miser bag rings currently
available in both gold and sterling silver plated finishes.
Manufactured by LACIS

LS79

LS74

LS73

LS67

LC88

LC87

LS80

LS75

LS72

LS68

LS69

LS78

LS58

LS81

[100]

WELDON'S
PRACTICAL BEAD-WORK.

(FIRST SERIES.)

HOW TO MAKE BEADED TASSELS, CUFFS, ORNAMENTS, SPRAYS, FRINGES, &c.

THIRTY-FOUR ILLUSTRATIONS.

PRACTICAL BEAD-WORK.

Now that the mania for using beads in such incalculable quantities on ladies' outdoor and indoor clothes shows no sign of abatement, and bids fair to continue for some time yet to come, ladies are beginning to devote their spare time to the ornamentation of panels, tabliers, waistcoats, cuffs, and collars for their dresses to suit their own fancy, and in colours corresponding with those of any particular gown. Nor is it simply for the decoration of their own wearing apparel that bead-work is to be recommended as an employment for ladies—one of its greatest advantages is, that for really good work there is always a market to be found; but it must be remembered that not the beading alone must be well done, but the mounting and lining also; and we can conscientiously advise nobody to undertake the work with a view of making it profitable unless she be fully competent to make it up when done. Although bead-work requires skill and some amount of patience, it is so different to ordinary embroidery that many who have not sufficient artistic taste to master the intricacies of art needlework in the more limited signification of the term, may yet succeed perfectly in this more mechanical style of work; and it is with the object of assisting this portion of the community of lady workers that the following practical hints on the subject of bead-work have been put to paper.

MATERIALS FOR BEAD-WORK.

ANOTHER great advantage possessed by bead-work is the large range of materials upon which it may be executed. Amongst the transparent fabrics are net, gauze, tulle, lace, muslin, while for those who prefer to work upon a firmer foundation, there are silk, velvet, plush, satin, besides cashmere and other soft woollens.

For threading the beads, long fine needles known as "straw" needles are pleasant to use where a number of beads are to be passed on at once, and may be had of several lengths and in various degrees of thickness. For bead embroidery "betweens" are more convenient than a longer make of needle. An extra needle may sometimes be useful if made by the worker herself of a short length of very fine wire. To make this, bend the wire like a little hook at one end and place it over a pin, hold both ends of wire firmly with the left hand, and with the right hand twist the pin once or twice so that it twists the wire also; when the wire is twisted close to the pin, take it out. This leaves a small loop which is to form the eye of the needle; cut off the short end of wire as close to the twisted part as possible. A needle such as this is often useful from the facility with which it may be bent to suit any shape of bead, and on an emergency it is often quite as handy as the firmer sorts of needles that are more often used.

There is great variety in the thread upon which the beads can be threaded, its selection, of course, depending upon the material on which the work is executed, as well as upon the size of the beads. As a general rule, nothing is better than silk twist, coarse or fine, according to circumstances. It is certainly more expensive, but keeps its colour better than any make of thread or cotton. Should it seem inclined to wear rough as the beads are passed over

No. 1.—A Simple Design for Beading.

it, a little wax will soon set this straight. Mecklenburg thread is, however, to be recommended for pieces of work that are not to be subjected to minute inspection.

For making passementerie, gimps, macarons, and such things, fine silk cord is required, which may be procured from any good trimming warehouse under the name of "case cord."

Fine and coarse wire, both covered and uncovered, and moulds of different shapes are also needed, and various other trifles of the same kind which will be alluded to hereafter as occasion arises.

Now a word as to the choice of the beads themselves. They should, for good work, always be chosen of the very best quality, as the inferior kinds are apt to be irregular both in colour and shape. Pearl beads more especially must be carefully chosen, while coarse, cheap jet is so heavy as to be almost unwearable when it is used in any great quantity. It is well to lay in a good stock of any fancy beads before commencing to work, as sometimes, if more be required, it is difficult and often impossible to match them again exactly. Most metal and fancy beads are sold in bunches and dozen bunches, larger and millinery beads in strands or strings, while the commoner coloured glass beads are sold by weight, either sorted into their various shades of colour, or as "mixed" or "pound" beads. Bugles are little used just now by themselves, but may very effectively be mingled with the round or cut-glass beads.

GENERAL DIRECTIONS FOR BEAD-WORK.

THE first thing to be done is to trace the pattern out on the material, and the method of doing this varies according to whether this material is transparent or opaque, and is with or without a raised pile. If velvet or any similar fabric is to be used, the pattern must be transferred to it by means of pouncing. This is done by drawing or tracing the design accurately on a sheet of firm cartridge paper with pen and ink, then laying it down upon a piece of house flannel, or an ironing blanket folded so that there are four thicknesses of it. With a very large needle for a pricker or a bonnet pin, prick holes firmly and regularly all over the outlines of the pattern. Place these holes very near together for small and intricate patterns, and further apart for straight lines and bolder designs. When this is done, lay the velvet with the right side uppermost on the blanket, then the pricked pattern with the rough side of the holes uppermost. Place leaden weights or large books to keep the velvet from slipping, and dust powdered chalk or charcoal, according to the colour of the material, over the paper. With a little pad of flannel or wash-leather, rub the chalk well over the pricked holes, then carefully remove the paper so as not to sprinkle the powder over the material, and the design should be found reproduced upon the velvet. Lay the pricked paper pattern by the side of the velvet, and with a fine paint-brush dipped in Chinese white, delicately connect the chalk dots with each other so as to render them more easily seen. If the beads are to be merely sprinkled at regular intervals over the design, the original holes pricked in the paper must be considered as each representing a bead, and on the velvet the dots only must be touched with paint, not connected into lines. Of course patterns may be transferred to cashmere and such materials either in this way or by the use of ordinary tracing-paper, but much trouble and time may be saved by the help of Briggs' patent transferring papers. It must, however, be understood that these useful patterns are of no use upon any material that will not bear the pressure of a warm flat iron. No choice must fall upon naturalistic flowers or fruits. The designs, to be quite successful, must be either geometric or purely conventional; and what to avoid in bead-work as applied to cushion covers, screens, and the like, may be learnt by a study of the gaudy flowers, glassy pet dogs, and similar elaborate handiwork, over which our grandmothers were accustomed to spend so much of their time and patience.

In beading upon net, crape, and such transparent materials, the design should be traced with ink upon pink or white glazed calico, or stout brown or cartridge paper, according to the colour of the fabric that is chosen. The net is tacked carefully and smoothly over the pattern, and the design followed without taking the stitches through to the calico. Madras muslin is a good material to use as a foundation for beading, and can be used for panels, collars, and vests of dresses. The designs on this material are often very good and more easy for an amateur to follow than are those upon the grenadine that we so often see used for mantles and dress trimmings. It must be borne in mind that when beading a design of sprays that are sprinkled at intervals over a thin foundation, the needle must not be slipped from place to place at the back of the work, but as each spray is finished the thread must be firmly

No. 3.—Smocking with Beads.

fastened off and a fresh beginning made at the next spray. It is surely scarcely necessary to explain that the reason for this is to avoid the unsightly appearance the line of thread between the sprays would have, showing through to the right side of a transparent material.

The idle way of working a pattern that is in the least degree similar to braiding is to thread the beads in a long string and to catch them down over the pattern, much as "couching" is done in artistic embroidery. The plan is mentioned here as one more example of what to avoid, for, except in rare instances, to be referred to hereafter, no worker who wishes to excel will follow this plan. In the best work the beads are each sewn on separately to the material, thus lessening the risk of losing perhaps a long string of them should the thread break. Whether working with small beads, or with large many-sided ones, or with bugles, it is best to thread one or two and to pass it along the thread until it is close to the material before putting the needle in again to the wrong side of the work. This will not only prevent the work from becoming puckered, but will make the stitches come so exactly in their proper places that the cotton or silk will be almost, if not entirely hidden. Tiny pieces of thread or silk showing beyond the holes of a bead are always a sure proof that the work has been done by an inexperienced hand.

Large pieces of satin, silk, or net, such as would be used for the front or panels of a skirt must be worked by preference in a frame. To most workers it is easier to work upon a large surface when it is thus firmly stretched, and for small pieces of work, such as lace, the wire frames of different shapes and sizes that are used for guipure d'art will be found very useful.

EFFECTIVE COLOURS FOR BEAD-WORK.

AMONGST the infinite variety of colours in which beads are made now-a-days it surely should be no difficult task to arrange effective combinations of shades, but a few such mixtures are mentioned here to help those workers who are able to carry out the suggestions of others and yet who are unable to originate ideas for themselves.

An uncommon mixture for a dinner dress is arranged of old-gold satin and steel beads; far prettier, however, are steel beads upon *vieux-rose*, pearl beads upon *eau de nil*, brown beads upon coral pink, Tosca upon blue, sapphire upon French grey, crimson upon fawn, peacock-blue upon *réséda*, olive upon mouse-colour, and coral pink upon cream-coloured material. Brown beads mixed with either gold thread or beads look well upon brown velvet, white crystal, satin or pearls upon white or cream satin. Pale pink, or blue Madras muslin for evening wear looks specially pretty when the design has been outlined with silver, moonlight, or crystal beads, mixed in with which are small drops and tassels made of larger beads of the same colours. Moonlight and sunlight, and iridescent beads of all sorts always look well upon any material of a dark

No. 2.—Beading with the Aid of Smocking Dots.

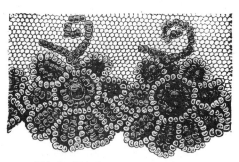

No. 4.—Edging worked on Net.

or neutral shade of colour. Metal beads may be had in three and sometimes four shades of the same colour, so the choosing of these to assort with any material should be by no means a difficult task.

No. 1.—A SIMPLE DESIGN FOR BEADING.

THIS simple little design for beading on cashmere or some similar material is useful from its simplicity alone, which is so great that with average care it may be worked without any trouble of transferring the pattern to the material. A straight line ruled with chalk on the cashmere is all that is necessary, and it will be seen by studying the illustration that the beads are sewn on in sets of three. Three at equal distances apart are laid along the straight chalk line, then sets of three are sewn on so as to slant from one end of each of these groups, then three more on the opposite side of the centre to correspond with them. That is all of which this little pattern consists. It will be specially useful just now for working with gold or silver beads along each side of a fancy *galon* such as is used so largely for the ornamentation of blotters, note-books, photo-screens, and other fancy goods. A variety may be made in it by the use of bugles for the centre, or it may be worked entirely in fancy beads if more convenient.

No. 2.—BEADING WITH THE HELP OF SMOCKING DOTS.

THE transferable patterns of honeycombing or smocking dots that are such a boon to workers of this particular style of work now-a-days, may also be applied very successfully to bead-work, as may be seen in the above illustration. Three kinds of beads are required for this, small cut jet ones, small, round, dull jet and larger cut jet beads about the size of a small pepper-corn. The work is commenced at a corner of the dotted portion of the material. After the end of the thread has been firmly fastened there, four dull jet beads are passed on to it. Then pick up the second dot from the top in the next row with a stitch, thread four beads, pick up the third dot in the next row, thread four beads, pick up the fourth dot in the fourth row, and continue to work thus diagonally across the material until the edge of the dotted portion is reached. Fasten off the thread. Miss one row of dots and begin again as before on the second dot below the one that was first picked up. Work diagonally across the material, and when all the rows have been worked that slant in this direction, begin again in the same way, and work a series of rows slanting in exactly the opposite way and intersecting those that were first worked. The worker will know she is right if she is careful in these rows always to pick up a dot that has been picked up in working the previous rows. When these are all done, the cashmere will have an appearance of being divided into squares as in quilting, with beads taking the place of the rows of stitching. In the

it is much more difficult to sew on more than two in such a manner as to destroy the regularity of the work.

Many of the varieties of smocking, besides the honeycomb pattern, may be thus worked, but there is no need to give directions for them in this place, as they have been already fully described in "Weldon's Practical Smocking."

No. 4.—EDGING WORKED ON NET.

THIS narrow beading pattern forms a light and pretty ornament for trimming hats and bonnets, and for fichus and collarettes. It is simply worked upon net, and requires three kinds of beads, pearls as large as a small pea, seed pearls, and small smoked pearl beads. This mixture looks specially well for such a piece of embroidery, but coloured, plomb, or Tosca beads look effective and pretty. Trace the design upon pink or white glazed cambric, and mark it out very distinctly with a pen and ink. Do not sew on more than two beads at a time, or a well-defined outline cannot be obtained. Trace the flowers with the small, white pearls, and fill them in with the smoked pearls. Add one of the larger pearls in the extreme centre of the flower. Take particular care not to let the stitches go through the glazed calico pattern. Any ends of thread must be left till the beading is finished before they can be fastened off on the wrong side. When all the net has been worked over the pattern, cut the tacking threads and lay a fresh piece of net over the calico, taking special care to make the pattern fit in exactly. Finally cut away the net along the three small scallops that form the lower edge of each flower, and see that the scissors do not snip the thread that holds the beads.

No. 5.—BEADED TRIMMING ON NET.

To work this very effective and elegant little trimming, three different kinds of beads are required, tiny round ones, large cut jet beads about the size of a

No. 7.—Beaded Cord.

No. 5.—Beaded Trimming on Net.

No. 8.—Fringe.

No. 6.—Simple Bead Trimming.

centre of each square there will be a smocking dot, and on this must be sewn one of the smaller cut jet beads. A larger cut jet bead must be sewn on at the point at which all the previous lines of dull jet beads intersect each other, also at the outer corners of the squares. In working this pattern, particular care must be taken not to draw or pucker the material at all, especially in putting on the lines of dull jet beads. Here, too, bugles or long cut jet beads are effective if used instead of the small, dull, jet ones. Net may be used in preference to an opaque material, but the dots in this case must be transferred to pink or white glazed calico, and the net tacked over it so that they show through plainly enough to be followed with the beading. Net, thus embroidered, is especially useful for stretching over the crown of a hat, or for the centre portion of a bag vest for the front of a dress.

No. 3.—SMOCKING WITH BEADS.

A PLEASANT and effective variation may be made in the ordinary honeycomb smocking pattern by introducing beads in the place of the ordinary silk stitches which are used to connect the pleats to form the honeycomb. In working with beads, the pleats must be first held together with one firm stitch, then a second stitch with a bead is made over the first one. A variety may be made in the beads, some of which are more effective than others for this purpose. Pearls always look well either on a black, white, or coloured material; coloured beads must be chosen to suit the fabric upon which they are used, while for mourning wear, round cut jet beads are most effective upon a dull, black silk foundation. No beads of a very small size should be chosen, or if small, two, or even four should be used instead of one at each pleat, but

small peppercorn, and small bugles. The design is drawn with pen and ink on pink or white glazed calico, which if not firm enough, may be still further strengthened by a lining of brown paper. The net is then tacked over this pattern, and particular care must be taken to get it absolutely straight, according to the grain of the calico and that of the net. Except in the case of the scallops which border the central pattern, each bead must be sewn on separately, and it must be passed right along the thread close to the work before the needle is put back again into the net. This will prevent the net from becoming at all puckered during the progress of the work.

No. 6.—SIMPLE BEAD TRIMMING.

THIS useful and effective little trimming requires only beads and thread. The drawing shows it in its most simple form, but it may, at the expense of a little more time and trouble, be made much more elaborate by weaving in coloured beads to form a pattern, and by working the different rows of various lengths to form a scallop, or by working one row only, and knotting a series of loops into the edge beads to form a fringe. Take two needlefuls of the thread double the length of the piece of trimming that is required, thread them each through a bead needle, double the thread in half, and knot all four ends together. Should the thread be very strong, it may be used singly. Pin the ends firmly down to a leaded pincushion. Thread one bead on the right hand strand, so that its tip points towards the lead cushion. Take the left hand needle in the right hand and the right hand needle in the left hand, draw both threads through the bead, pushing it as near as it will go to the knot at the end of the threads. Thread two beads on the right hand strand and one on the left hand strand. Pass the left hand strand through the second bead of the right hand one and draw the three beads evenly right up to the end. This forms a sort of diamond-shaped pattern. Again pass two beads on to the right hand strand and one on the left, and cross the left hand one through the second bead so that it becomes the right hand strand. Continue thus until the piece of trimming is long enough. Fasten off tightly by knotting the ends of thread together close to the last bead. The pattern is to be made wider by joining on another row made in a similar manner to the first, but using two beads instead of three.

Leave the first part of the trimming fixed to the cushion, prepare the two needlefuls of thread as before, tie the ends together, and pin them to the cushion beside the first part of the trimming. Pass one bead on to the right hand strand and cross the left hand one through it. Thread two beads on the right hand strand, pass the left hand needle through the first side bead of the right hand side of the piece of trimming, then through the second bead on the right hand strand. Draw the beads up as before, then again thread two beads on the right hand strand, pass the left hand needle through the next side bead of the trimming, then through the second bead on the right hand strand, and continue thus until the second piece of trimming is as long as the first piece.

When once the method of making this trimming is grasped, it will be seen in what an infinite number of ways it may be varied. For a piece of work of this sort, be careful to choose beads that are as regular as possible both in size and shape. Draw the threads up so that the various sets of beads rest evenly and freely against each other, but yet are not so near as to fret and break the threads, or look loose and slovenly when the trimming is in use.

No. 7.—BEADED CORD.

FAN girdles may be very satisfactorily made in the way just described for a trimming, and look specially well made of pearl beads of rather a large size. Round cord and chains for looping up the drapery of a dress, for holding the muff in winter, or ornamenting the edge of the brim of a hat, may also be made very ingeniously of these flat bands of trimming. A piece of ordinary silk cord is required for them, of such a width as to encircle the cord when folded round it, leaving only the size of a bead all down between its two edges. Probably from four to six rows of beads will be required. Thread two bead needles as before, lay the cord over the bead web, and fasten the two bead needles to the pincushion. Thread a bead on one strand, cross the other through it and draw it up, take the right hand needle through the first side bead of the trimming on the right hand side, and the left hand needle through the corresponding bead on the left hand side of the trimming, thread one bead on one of the strands, and cross the other strand through it. Continue thus to draw the sides of the trimming together over the cord until a sufficient length is completed, then tie all the ends of the strands of thread together and fasten off.

Tassels may be attached to the end of the cord, or a bar to one end and a swivel to the other, should it be intended for use as a watch-chain.

Other bead chains, that are to a novice the same as these in general appearance, may be made of very small, round black beads, which are all threaded upon black purse silk. With a fine steel crochet hook make a chain of ten stitches, join it in a circle, and place it over a slender pencil, a stout knitting needle, a round netting mesh, or any other round stick that will fit this ring. Crochet round and round in double crochet from the inside of the circle and slip a bead close up to every stitch before drawing the silk through. Continue thus, pushing up the pencil as the work grows longer and requires it. Add a bar and swivel.

In the days when fan girdles were worn, they were often very prettily made in this way, of sparkling beads.

A third way of making a cord or chain of beads requires a good deal of patience, but many people would consider it less fidgety to make one in this way than to crochet it. The materials required are:—fine purse silk, small round beads, a stout knitting needle, a circular piece of firm cardboard measuring five inches across with a hole cut in the centre about half an inch across, and the outer edge cut into twelve scallops (it is well to cut a paper pattern of this first, as it is somewhat troublesome otherwise to get it regular), twelve small pieces of card to serve as silk winders, an empty reel, and a round, deep box, a round vase or a jam pot.

Cut some purse silk into twelve lengths, each rather longer than the chain is to be when finished, and thread a good quantity of beads on each. Wind each round one of the cardboard winders, and either roll each one up in a piece of tissue paper, or better still, pass an elastic band over them to keep them from becoming unwound. Wind a good long length of silk round the empty reel and secure the end in the notch. Tie all the ends together with the one on the reel and put the knot through the hole made in the round piece of cardboard. Run a long knitting needle through the knot so that it will serve as a bar and prevent it from slipping through the hole. Place this circle on the top of the round box, needle downwards. Unwind from the winders enough silk to enable them to hang over the edge of the circle of cardboard, each resting in one of the twelve notches between the scallops. Push a bead upon each of these strands as far as it will go into the centre. Then take the reel, undo some of the silk and twist it round each of the twelve threads, stroking the twists close to the beads with the help of a needle or large pin. When every thread has been thus encircled, push up another set of beads and twist the silk round as before. When about eight rounds have been worked, push the stout knitting needle into the middle of this little piece of cord, so as to form a centre round which the rest of the work may be carried. It will go right through the central hole of the card, partly into the box below and will keep upright without any difficulty. Slide the needle up as the work progresses, and when the chain is long enough, run the ends of thread with a fine needle through the beads that were worked on in the last three or four rounds. Then undo the knot and finish off the other end in the same way and cut off the ends close down to the work.

No. 8.—FRINGE.

THIS novel and pretty fringe needs for its manufacture three kinds of beads only—two sorts of small, round beads, say dull and bright jet, and some large round fancy beads of any kind that is convenient. The heading of the fringe is made first. Two strong threads are required, each the length that is needed. Tie the ends together and pin them down to a heavy cushion. Pass both strands through one of the dull jet beads, thread a bright jet bead

No. 9.—Design for Collar in Bead-Work.

No. 10.—Design for Cuff in Bead-Work.

No. 11.—Spray for Millinery.

No. 12.—Beaded Osprey.

on each strand, thread a dull bead on the right hand strand, pass the left hand one through it so that they cross and change places, draw them up closely, thread a bright bead on each, cross them again through a dull bead, and continue until a sufficiently long piece has been made. For the drops, pass a strong piece of thread through one of the cut jet beads of the heading, draw it through until the bead is in the middle of it, thread a bright bead on each strand, cross both strands through a dull bead exactly as when the heading was made, and continue thus until there are eight dull beads on, then pass both strands through one bright bead, one dull bead, one bright bead, one large fancy bead, one bright bead. Tie the thread here firmly between the last bead and the fancy one, run it through three or four beads, including the fancy one, and cut it off short. The next drop is worked into the third bright bead of the heading, thus leaving two beads between each drop.

Nos. 9 and 10.—DESIGN FOR COLLAR AND CUFF IN BEAD-WORK.

THIS collar and cuff may be worked in several different ways. The design is one which would lend itself admirably to a mixture of embroidery and

No. 11.—SPRAY FOR MILLINERY.

THIS spray, which is intended to be mixed in with the loops of ribbon in the front of a hat or bonnet, requires making up on wire to stiffen it and to make it stand upright in the now approved style. The original, of which a portion only is shown in the illustration, is made of a mixture of black and crystal beads, but any other two colours, such as gold and bronze, or silver and crimson, may be used, or the spray may be made in one only, such as jet or garnet, with an almost equally good result. Cut a piece of wire twenty-four inches long, and pass on thirty-three beads, alternately one of each colour that has been chosen for the spray. Place the beads quite in the middle of the length of wire and bend it in half. Hold the two ends of the wire in the left hand about half an inch below the beads, hold the beads in the right hand and twist them neatly three or four times, thus making a small loop with a twisted stalk. Thread twenty-four beads in the same way upon one of the ends of the wire, twist this as the first loop was twisted, then thread twenty-four beads on the other piece of wire, and make a third loop. Twist the two lengths of wire together for about half an inch to make a central stem, then make another pair of loops. Be careful in making these side loops not to push the beads along the wire as far as they will go before beginning to twist, but allow half an inch of wire beyond the beads, or the wire will not have "play" enough,

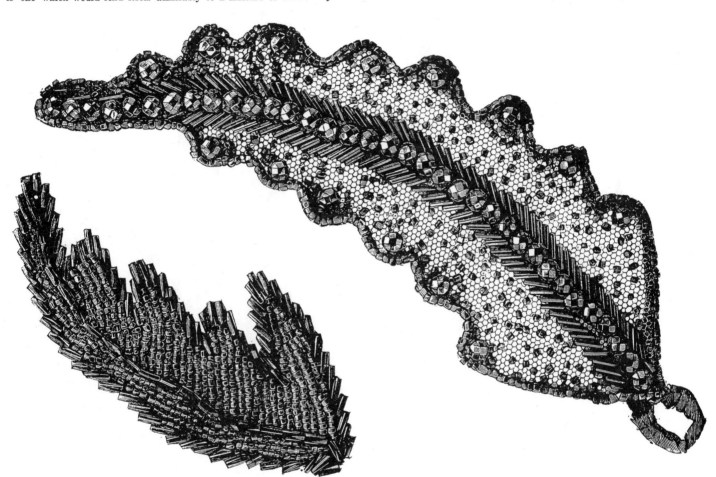

No. 14.—Wing for a Hat or Bonnet.

No. 13.—Transparent Leaf for Millinery.

beads, the outlines of the feathers of which it consists being followed with stitches worked in coarse silk and filled in with beads. The small isolated designs which are here and there mingled with the feathers would look best if executed with thick satin stitch embroidery. Should beads only be preferred, the outlines of the feathers would be very effective when followed with small bugles, and the centre stems marked out with tiny round cut beads. Net may be used as a foundation for the work, but better still is silk or velvet. If the latter material be chosen, the collar and cuffs would have a specially good effect if carried out in iridescent metallic blue beads, with a judicious mixture of gold beads. Much of the newer bead embroidery has a considerable admixture of tinsel, and in such a design as the one before us we should recommend the outlines of the feathers being worked with tinsel cord, and the centres and stems filled up with beads. For working, the design may be transferred straight to the material itself, if it be a firm fabric, such as velvet or silk, with the help of tracing and transferring paper; but if net is to be used, the design must be copied on to a firm piece of white paper and the net tacked over this.

The amateur must be careful to line and finish off the collar and cuffs, when embroidered, in a workmanlike, neat manner, more especially if they are to be used occasionally to freshen up a dress, not made up on the gown itself.

and in consequence will, perhaps, break off. When this happens there is nothing for it but to begin again from the very beginning and to profit by experience. Continue to make as many of these side loops as the length of wire will allow, probably about seven on each side. Twist the two ends of the wire together. In mounting such a spray into a group for the front of a bonnet it is well to vary the number of leaves, and to have some sprays with seven in all, others with eleven, thirteen, or less. They must be wired together to form a large upstanding group in somewhat of a fan shape, but long wreaths of them have a really charming and uncommon appearance when laid down each side of a bonnet. With a velvet crown, ribbon strings, and bow for the front, and these sprays for the side, scarcely any other trimming is required to make a really serviceable little bonnet. The shapes of the beads may be varied, and bugles or seed-shaped beads mixed in with the round ones if preferred, while a bead of an extra large size may be slipped on to the twisted wire stalk between each pair of side leaves should it be considered necessary, but this is rather apt to detract from the light appearance that is one of the charms of these little sprays.

No. 12.—BEADED OSPREY.

THE feather ospreys that are always such a becoming addition to the appearance of a bonnet are, as most ladies know to their cost, far from being durable, especially when worn in all weathers. The bead osprey figured here has almost as good an effect, with the great advantage of being entirely uninfluenced by rain, snow, or fog. To make a good, full spray, about twenty to thirty pieces of fine wire are needed, varying in length from four to six inches. Small cut jet beads and fancy silver beads look pretty together, but any other mixture of colour may be used; and it can be readily understood that the smaller the beads the lighter and more elegant will be the appearance of the osprey. Thread a silver bead upon one of the pieces of wire, and push it along until it is within a quarter of an inch of the end. Bend the wire, and twist the short end as closely and tightly as possible round the longer length

No. 20.—The Marguerite Vest.

of wire quite close to the bead. Then pass on alternately three black beads and one silver bead, and it will be found that if the twist has been deftly done, the beads will pass over it close up to the first bead, and it will then be entirely hidden. Leave a piece of wire about an inch long at the other end without any beads upon it. The lengths of beads thus made are wired together at the end, and thus is completed the simplest of all ornaments for use in millinery. It will be seen that the sprays in the illustration have been slightly bent in order to economise space.

No. 13.—TRANSPARENT LEAF FOR MILLINERY.

THIS elegant leaf is best adapted for the ornamentation of a lace hat or bonnet, as its beauty consists in its transparency and apparent lightness. It may either be made of jet beads of various kinds, as in the example, or of pearl and crystal beads for use in a cream-coloured bonnet. The choice of beads for this leaf is much limited owing to the very few colours in which stiff net is to be procured. The shape of the leaf must be carefully cut out in the net and outlined with black covered wire, two ends of which, each about an inch and a half long, are left and twisted together to form the stalk. A row of small cut jet beads threaded upon wire is sewn all round the edges, the stitches which secure this being taken over the wired edges of the leaf. A large cut jet bead is sewn on in each curve of the leaf. Run a line of black cotton to mark the centre of the leaf, from the stalk to the tip, and on each side of this sew on a row of bugles so arranged as to slant from this centre as fish-bones do from the spine. Leave a space of half-an-inch up the middle between each row of bugles, but put them as closely as possible one over the other. It will be found necessary to put only one row of bugles when about within an inch and a half of the tip. Thread about three dozen of the larger cut jet beads on wire. Twist one end of the wire round the stalk of the leaf and sew the line of large beads along the centre of the leaf between the two rows of bugles. It will now be seen that the reason why one row only of the bugles was sewn on near the tip was to gain space for this central string of the larger beads. Finish off the end of wire at the top by pushing it through to the wrong side and sewing it firmly down. Sew a number of the smaller beads singly, dotting them about at irregular intervals over the remaining portions of the net, and finally twist a strip of black tissue round the stalk of the leaf.

Butterflies for ornamenting headdresses and caps may be made also on much the same general plan as this leaf, but using, of course, brightly-

No. 15.—Cor

No. 16.—Double Ornamen

coloured beads for them. The feelers are contrived by threading the smallest-sized beads upon a piece of fine wire, then bending the wire back, and threading it again through the beads, missing the one that was threaded last. This bead should be a trifle larger than the others, and the space of an eighth of an inch left between it and them, so as to give the wire "play" and room enough for the twist. When the beads have all been threaded, give the wire a twist or two between this bead and the others. This will make the last and largest bead simulate the knot that forms one of the chief characteristics of these insects. Should the butterfly be very small, it is better to make its feelers of a double strand of wire tightly twisted and with one bead only at the extreme tip. The body of the insect is best made of a long narrow roll of cotton wool or wadding covered with black velvet, if a large creature is to be made; and with thin silk, as being less bulky, if a small one. Beads are threaded either upon wire or upon stout thread, and the strand is twisted round and round the body and held in place by frequent stitches carried through it. It is better, for the smaller insects, to push the beads along the thread so that they are all on the upper side of the body. To do this effectually, a sufficient number of beads to stretch across the body must be threaded on a piece of thread, the end of which is fastened at one end of the body. The needle is then passed through the body and out at the side of the place from which it started. Other rows of beads are carried across in the same way until the whole of the body is covered up.

No. 14.—WING FOR A HAT OR BONNET.

THIS wing is made on a slightly different principle to that on which the leaf No. 13 already described is formed, as the whole of the background is covered up with beads, but additional brightness is added here also by the use of bugles or long cut jet beads. The shape must be cut out accurately in stiff black net, and this is made opaque by covering it with thin, black silk. Sew covered black wire all round the edges to stiffen them and leave two ends about an inch and a half long at the lower end, which must be twisted together to serve as the quill of the wing. Sew bugles round the edges in a slanting direction as evenly as possible, and let them project a trifle beyond the edge in order that they may hide the wire. Join the thread at the base of the wing and pass on to it a sufficient number of small, cut jet beads to reach from the base to the tip of the first point. Pass the needle and thread through to the wrong side and work back to the place from whence the line of beads started, catching them down here and there with a stitch brought up from the wrong side, then lay on a second row of beads in the same manner and continue to work thus until the whole of one side of the wing, from the edge to the centre, is filled up. Work in the same way along the other side of the middle, leaving a space between the two sets of beads just the width of a bugle. Now thread upon fine wire about nineteen or twenty of the same bugles as those which are sewn along the edges, and lay them down the wing to form the centre shaft. Sew the end of the wire at the tip of the wing firmly down on the wrong side and twist the other end round the stem. Catch down this line of bugles in the middle with a few stitches and finally twist thin black paper or narrow ribbon round the quill to make all neat and tidy. Wings similar to this may be made of almost any colour, but garnet beads are particularly successful when thus applied. Whatever colour be chosen, the net shape must be

Foundation for No. 16.

for Dresses or Mantles.

covered with thin silk to match, as coloured nets are not stiff enough to be used for this purpose.

Nos. 15 and 16.—DOUBLE ORNAMENT.

To make this ornament, a considerable variety of beads is required: a quantity of small cut jet beads, two dozen cut jet beads the size of a small currant, twenty-six long and pointed beads about three-quarters of an inch long, and pierced at the upper and blunter end only, fourteen round flat, cut jet beads, pierced through the centre and known as mitres, two of these a size larger, a dozen small black wooden moulds hollow in the middle, and several yards of fine "case" cord. The two flat ornaments are made first, then the drops, and lastly the connecting lengths of cord. The cord foundations, of one of which an illustration is given (No. 15), must be made first of the case cord, which is firm and wiry, and can readily be bent into any shape. In making a foundation for passementerie of this kind, it is well first to draw the design carefully on a piece of stout paper, and to twist the cord into the desired form by laying it frequently down on the pattern, and keeping the strands, thus shaped, in place by stitches taken through the middle of the cord. Care is needed, especially at first, to keep the strands of cord perfectly flat, but the knack required will soon be gained, and after a little practice the

worker will be able to arrange these cord foundations without the trouble of sketching a paper pattern. The work may be described as braiding without a

No. 18.—Passementerie Ornament.

background. In the upper part of this particular ornament the cord is twisted as flatly as possible into seven circles, which it can be understood are to serve to hold the seven flat beads. Below these, two strands of cord are wide enough when sewn together, to form the foundation, but lower down it widens a little, and three strands are needed. It is advisable to prepare both these cord foundations at once, as the first one is easier to copy before any beads are sewn on to it, and it is moreover less difficult to make them both alike when they are in this stage of progress.

Now begin to cover the foundation with beads, commencing in the centre, thread three of the smaller cut jet beads, pass them along the thread till they are close down to the work, lay them across the strands of cord in a slanting direction, hold them down under the thumb of the left hand, and pass the needle through the strands of cord back to the side of the first of the three beads. Draw the thread up closely. Thread three more beads, hold them down in the same way by the side of the others, and continue thus until the whole of the upper surface of the cord is covered with these short lines of beads, giving, as it were, the appearance of a flattened jet cord. Notice that

Draw the thread up closely, but not so tightly as to prevent the drop from hanging well. Secure it in place with a buttonhole stitch worked into the edge of the foundation, and pass the needle on to the next place, from whence a drop is to hang. Each drop, it will be observed, consists of a long string of beads with a loop at the end, from which hangs a pointed bead. When all the drops are made, the wooden moulds must next be covered with beads. Knot the thread firmly on the mould first, by passing it through the middle and then tying it tightly. Start from one end of the mould, thread six of the smaller beads, and for this position they must be chosen perfectly regular both in size and shape, pass them along the mould, then push the needle through the hole in the mould and out at the other end, thread six more beads, put the needle through again and continue thus until the mould is entirely covered with beads. About fourteen sets of six will probably be required, and they must be arranged with judgment so that they set side by side quite flat, and do not overlap each other at all. When all the moulds have been thus covered,

No. 21.—Tassel.

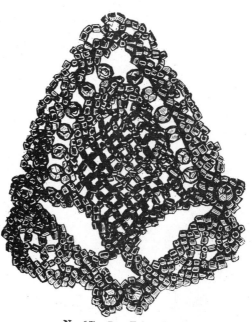

No. 17.—Jet Trimming.

No. 22.—Beaded Button.

No. 19.—Beaded Galon.

the upper portion of the foundation, being narrower than the lower, will require two beads to cover it instead of three. Do not take the lines of beads quite into the centre, as the large mitre will need a flat cord foundation upon which to rest. In really good passementerie of this sort, which, by the way, is always hand-made abroad, and often by men, scarcely any stitches show on the wrong side, as they are all taken through the middle of the cord, not over it. The seven flat mitres are, of course, firmly sewn down to the flat circles prepared for them, the larger ones occupying the extreme centres of the two ornaments.

The drops must be attached to the four beaded and corded loops found at the lower edge of the ornament, four being placed on each of the two middle loops, one between these two loops and two on each of the side loops, thus making thirteen in all. Fasten an end of strong thread in the proper place on the ornament, and pass on twenty-six small cut jet beads, one long pointed one and five small ones, pass the needle upwards through the beads that were threaded first, missing the five that are nearest to the long-pointed bead.

make the cord which connects the two ornaments join the thread, which must be rather longer than double the length that the cord is to be made, to the middle of the first jetted loop below the first mitres on the beaded foundation. Thread thirteen small beads, one large cut jet bead, pass the thread through one of the moulds, thread one large cut jet bead, thirteen small beads, one large cut bead, pass the thread through a mould, thread one large cut jet bead, thirteen small beads, one large cut bead, pass the thread through a mould, thread one large cut jet bead, thirteen small beads. Sew the thread firmly into the first loop below the mitres on the second ornament, so that it corresponds exactly with the first one. Pass the needle through the last threaded small bead, thread on the same strand thirteen small beads, pass the thread through the first cut jet bead, mould, and second cut jet bead of last row, thread thirteen small beads, pass the thread through the third cut bead, mould, and fourth cut bead of last row, thread thirteen small beads, pass the thread through the fifth cut jet bead, mould, and sixth cut jet bead of last row, thread thirteen small beads and pass the needle through the last of the thirteen small beads that were threaded first in the last row. Secure the thread firmly to the edge of the loop at the place from whence it started.

This completes one cord, three of which are required for this ornament. The second one is secured between the same loop and the next on the ornament, and the third one in the middle of the next loop. The second cord is made in exactly the same way, but is rather longer owing to the use of four moulds instead of three, while the third cord is longer still, and requires five moulds. The fastening on of this third cord completes the ornament, which is as handsome a decoration as anyone could desire either for the front of a jacket in the fashionable style, or for looping across a panel at the side of a gown.

four beads each and which are sewn on at intervals round the cord. This is a particularly well defined and easy design to follow, and hence is well adapted for a beginner to try her skill upon.

No. 18.—PASSEMENTERIE ORNAMENT.

THIS ornament, like the preceding one, is made up upon a foundation of cord, which must be prepared first. Notice that to do this well a beginning must be made, using two strands of cord together, in the centre of one of the round sides of the ornament, and that two lines of cord are carried down to make the three-pointed flat portion at the bottom, and from which are hung three tassels. Then the same two pieces of cord are carried up to match the other side, and are twisted round to form a second circle. A third strand of cord is added afterwards to widen the lower portion of the ornament. A fresh piece of cord must be taken for the upper part and

No. 23.—Bonnet or Hat Crown.

No. 17.—JET TRIMMING.

THIS jet trimming is useful for many purposes and has one great advantage not always to be found in such things—this is, that each vandyke is made separately, hence one may be detached from the others without any damage and used with a drop at the tip as a tassel, or three with drops can be used as epaulettes, so that all these minor ornaments will match the border of the drapery of the dress, which perhaps consists of a row of these patterns. Thus the patchwork and incomplete appearance that is often caused by the use of bead trimming of several different patterns is entirely obviated. The design itself calls for no special remark as much of it is filled in the same manner as the passementerie ornament before figured. It is, of course, made up upon a cord foundation covered with beads, and three of the spaces are filled in with a network as described in No. 18. Larger, single cut jet beads fill in the open spaces between two rows of cord and are dotted about in other places on the trimming. The lower edge is finished with a series of loops of

twisted at the extreme top into four flat circles which are to serve as a foundation for the four mitres.

Six kinds of beads are required, a quantity of small cut jet beads, three long four-sided beads pierced through the middle, and which are to form the heads of the tassels, two large cut jet beads somewhat of an oval shape and about the size of a small rose fruit, about three dozen small round cut jet beads as large as a peppercorn, one long cut bead pointed at each end, for the centre of the ornament near the top, and four small round mitres. The beads are sewn on the cord in a slanting direction two at a time, in the upper part of the ornament, three at a time in the lower half. The circles of cord at the sides are separated by closely set rows each of two beads, which are sewn on on the wrong side so that when looked at from the front, they are considerably depressed and so help to throw the corded portion into higher relief. The centre is occupied by the long cut jet bead, and the cord above it well covered with beads, which are threaded first and are kept down by a stitch between every two. The flat circles at the top of all are filled by the four mitres, which are surrounded by a single ring of beads only. The corded and beaded lower portion of the ornament has a number of the smallest sized beads sewn about a quarter of an inch apart, on the outer edge of the cord foundation, and the broad leaf-like shape itself is filled in with a network of the small beads. The beading for this is commenced at the top in the point, and just a trifle to the side of it. The beads are threaded in sets of three, the thread between each set of three in the next row being passed through the second bead of a set in the previous row. Before commencing this, it is as well to practise upon a rough foundation when the general idea of this network will soon be grasped, but the slope of the space to be filled up necessitates a slight variation being made in the numbers of the beads to be threaded at the sides, and this makes it impossible to lay down hard and fast rules concerning the exact numbers of the beads to be used at the sides of each row. To make the upper and shorter pair of drops, join on the thread at the bottom and in the middle of one of the circular patterns above the leaf. Thread one small cut bead, one larger one, twenty-one small ones, one very large cut bead, twenty-one small ones. Pass the thread through the tenth and the first of these last twenty-one beads, through the large bead, through five of the small ones, through the first one (next the smaller round cut bead), and through the single cut jet bead, draw the thread up closely and secure it in the cord at the place from whence it started. For

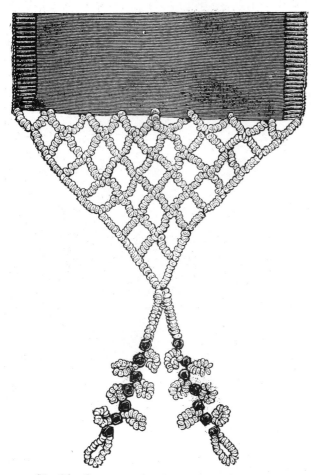

No. 24.—Ornament for End of Sash or Ribbon.

each tassel make a large knot at the end of a piece of thread, and thread one of the second sized cut beads, paying particular attention that the knot is large enough not to slip through the second hole in the bead, then thread forty small beads. Prepare thirty-six of these strands, twelve for each tassel, tie them firmly at the upper end and cut off all the threads but two or perhaps three. Pass these through one of the four-sided beads which are to form the head of the tassel, and the bead being wider at the bottom than at the top, will slip over the tied portion and hide it, pass the three threads through one of the second sized beads, then through one of the smallest and secure them firmly into one of the points of the lower portion of the ornament.

A piece of passementerie, such as this, looks particularly well when it is arranged with coloured beads to decorate a dress or mantle.

No. 19.—BEADED GALON.

THIS handsome galon may be taken as a very good type of those that are so largely used just now to trim the collars and cuffs of dress bodices, or the crowns and brims of hats. The model from which the accompanying wood-cut was prepared was worked entirely in red, two shades of garnet beads being used. A design is first of all either traced or drawn with pen and ink

upon a cotton or linen foundation of the prevailing colour of the beads—yellow for gold beads, grey for steel, and red for garnet. A pattern must be chosen of such a character as will allow the material beyond the outlines of the embroidery to be cut away, leaving the remaining portions to touch each other, and so keep the design together. Many patterns that are prepared at our fancy shops for reproduction in Guipure or Renaissance embroidery will serve equally well for this purpose. Follow all the lines with chain-stitch worked in coloured silk to accord with the beads. Thread the beads on a long thread, and sew them down, each one separately, over the cotton foundation, covering the spaces of the design entirely, between the lines of chain-stitch. When the whole pattern is covered with beads, take some embroidery paste and spread it evenly all over the back of the work. Place a sheet of tissue paper over the paste, and press it down with a cloth so that it will adhere well to every portion of the embroidery. Set it aside under heavy and even pressure until it is perfectly dry, then, with a sharp pair of scissors with good points, cut away the material between the lines of the pattern. A good embroidery paste for this purpose is made as follows: Put three dessert-spoonfuls of flour into a basin and mix enough cold water with it to make a stiff paste, perfectly smooth, and free from lumps. Take a quarter of a pint of boiling water, and while it is still on the fire, add a piece of resin the size of a pea, and which has been previously well powdered, and pour in the paste. Let it boil up several times, take it off the fire, and stir it continually until cold.

By sewing down each bead separately and using the paste carefully, this trimming is made so strong that it will bear cutting without losing more than one or two beads, which drop off at once, and the dilapidation spreads no further. This is always a sign by which good work may be distinguished from bad. In using steel beads very little paste must be spread over the work, and that very evenly distributed, or the surplus quantity will ooze through to the right side, and will tend to rust the beads. For this purpose the beads should be chosen as small and round as possible, and the pattern should repeat itself at intervals, thereby rendering it more easy to follow by an amateur worker.

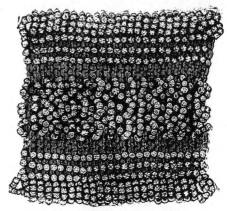

No. 25.—Knitted and Beaded Cuff.

No. 20.—THE MARGUERITE VEST.

AN effective way of working this vest is with black, silver, and gold beads. The black beads are used for the stems and leaves, the silver ones for the marguerites, and the gold beads for the eyes of the flowers. If preferred, it would look extremely effective when executed in beads of all one colour. The flowers should be entirely filled in with beads, the leaves merely outlined and veined with them. Single lines of beads form the stems.

The design may be worked either upon a piece of the material of which the dress itself is made, or it may be carried out upon silk or satin. If net be used, it will require lining with silk and carefully making up, a cascade of lace would be an improvement if carried down one, or both sides, but so much has been already said that will apply here also that we will leave this simple yet effective little design to speak for itself, feeling certain that no difficulty can be found in working it.

No. 21.—TASSEL.

THE head of this tassel is prepared first, the loops and drops being added afterwards. Procure an oblong mould that is hollow in the centre and covered with black silk. Thread a needle with strong black thread, and fasten it at one end of the mould, pass the needle through the centre to the opposite end, thread seven large round or cut jet beads, push them along the thread, and put the needle in again at the opposite end of the mould to that at which it last came out, draw it out at the other end, thread seven more beads and continue working thus over the mould until it is covered with beads. Care must be taken to let these beads set evenly and not too close, or one will spoil the other and spoil the neat appearance of the tassel. Fasten off the thread firmly by making a few stitches into the silk covering of the mould. To make the drops take a long piece of thread, pass on eight beads, push them to the middle and pass the needle through the two first; this makes a sort of little loop. Make four of these loops, taking care that they are close together. Pass both ends of the thread through a round cut jet bead a size larger than that used for the head of the tassel. Divide the threads again, and pass six beads on each. Pass both threads through one bead. Make four loops again, as before, two on each thread, but put ten beads on instead of eight, and pass both threads through one, instead of through two beads. Continue thus, and repeat from * until there are three sets of loops and three large beads. Finally, thread four beads on each thread, and knot the ends firmly together. This finishes one drop, of which two are required. To fix them to the body of the tassel, draw the thread through the mould, thread twelve beads on three of the threads, and twenty on the fourth. Take the threads back through the mould to the drop end of the tassel, and there fasten them off very firmly. The longer loop must in particular be fastened strongly, as it has to hold the whole weight of the tassel when it is in use.

No. 22.—BEADED BUTTON.

WITH the present style of dress a large button is often needed to, apparently, button back a lapel or revers on a redingote, but as it is often difficult to procure a beaded button for this purpose, the accompanying one has been figured to show how it is possible, with a little ingenuity, for the amateur worker to arrange one to suit her own fancy. A large flat button mould must be procured, or should there be any difficulty in so doing, one may be manufactured either from a bung or from four or five circles of cardboard, each with a small hole in the exact centre. These are laid one over the other, and covered with a piece of thin silk quite tightly and smoothly.

a smaller size. The beads should set as flatly as possible, and here the advantage of a cardboard mould will be recognised, as a stitch can here and there be put through mould and all, and will serve to keep the loops of beads in place. A similar network of small beads, as can be easily understood, may also be used to cover the head of a tassel, or a large mould that is required at intervals, perhaps, the length of a cord.

No. 23.—BONNET OR HAT CROWN.

THE general method of working a bonnet or hat crown similar to the one figured, is much the same as that already detailed for other pieces of embroidery upon net, but in this case bugles only are required, though the design is one which would lend itself well to a mixture of beads of various shapes and sizes. The pattern, too, is such as will allow of several beads being threaded on a single strand, and sewn down with a stitch between each bead in braiding fashion. In passing from one leaf to the next the stalk must be worked, and the thread, when the leaves are done, must be broken off and joined on again to work the flower in the centre, as on so thin a substance as net it cannot be passed from place to place across the back of the work.

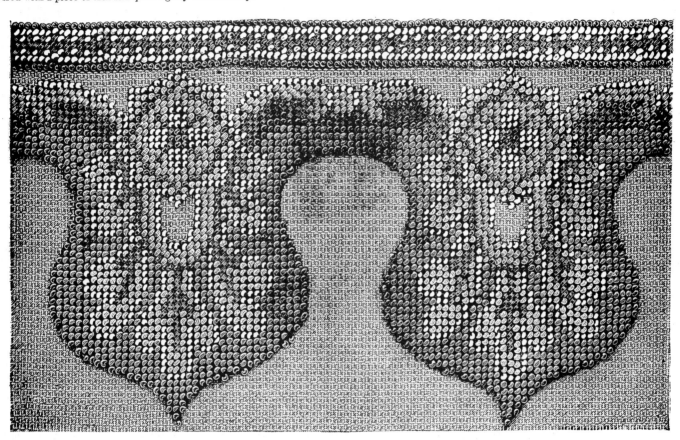

No. 26.— Bead Work on Canvas.

Four kinds of beads are used in the model—small cut jet beads, two sizes of round cut jet beads, and one raised, many-sided jet bead for the extreme centre. Join a piece of very strong thread to the edge of the button mould, and pass on to it a sufficient number of beads to reach round the button. Sew them firmly round the edge, placing a stitch between every two beads. **2nd round**—Thread five beads, pass the needle through the following fourth bead of the outer ring, thread five beads again, pass the needle through the fourth following bead as before, and repeat this until the end of the round. **3rd round**—Pass the needle through the middle bead of one of the loops of five beads of the last round, thread one of the smaller round cut jet beads, pass the needle through the middle bead of the next loop, and continue thus all round. **4th round**—Pass the needle through one of the larger beads of the last round, thread five beads, pass the needle through the second following large bead, and repeat all round. **5th round**—Pass the needle through the middle bead of one of the loops of the last round, thread five beads, pass the needle through the middle bead of the next loop, thread five beads again, and continue to the end of the round. **6th round**—Pass the needle through the middle bead of one of the loops of the last round, thread one of the larger round cut jet beads, pass the needle through the middle bead of the next loop, thread a larger bead, and continue till the end of the round is reached. Draw the network thus made up closely, and in the extreme centre sew on firmly the one raised fancy bead. This completes the button.

These directions apply to a button that measures nearly two inches across, but may be easily adapted to a similar ornament, if one be desired, of

No. 24.—ORNAMENT FOR THE END OF SASH OR RIBBON.

Specially Designed.

THIS ornament serves the double purpose of adding weight to the end of a sash, so that it keeps well down in its place, and of finishing off the raw edges which are so apt to become frayed and untidy by much wear. For ends of velvet ribbon such an ornament is a special improvement, as we all know how apt these are to curl up and crease. The network of beads at the upper part of the ornament may be made of any width to suit the width of the ribbon. The wider this is the longer will be the vandyke in proportion, and the tassels at the tip will have to be made longer or shorter accordingly.

Hem the end of the sash or ribbon to which the ornament is to be affixed, and fasten a long thread at one corner. Thread upon this thirteen beads. This is the number used in the model where the ribbon is three inches and a-half wide, and the beads rather flattened in form. For a narrow ribbon five beads will be quite sufficient. Loop the thread into the edge of the hem at a distance of about half an inch. Thread thirteen beads again, and sew them again into the edge at the distance of another half inch. Continue thus all along the ribbon. At the end pass the needle through the last seven beads, and work back, threading thirteen beads for each loop, and passing the thread through the seventh bead of each loop in succession of the last row. At the end pass the needle through the seven beads that were last threaded, and continue as before. When a small piece has been done, it will be seen that each row is shorter than the last, and as the work progresses the eighth row will be found to consist of one loop only, and into this the tassel has to be worked. Pass the needle through the six beads of this loop that were threaded last. Thread thirteen small beads, one larger one, thirteen small, one larger, thirteen small, one larger, thirteen small, one larger, until there are five of the larger-sized beads on the thread, then twenty small ones. Pass the needle back through the large beads only, thread thirteen small ones and draw the thread up closely, but not so tightly that the little loops do not hang well, then pass it through one bead of the loop from which the tassel started, and make another drop in the same way. When this is done, pass the thread through the remaining six beads of the loop, and fasten off firmly. Run in any ends of thread there may be through the beads, so that they are quite hidden. Three, or even five drops may be added, if preferred, or they may be placed all down the sides of the ornament.

A white sash for evening wear, finished with one of these ornaments, worked with pearl beads of two sizes, forms a pleasing addition to a white dress, while they are equally pretty for children's use, made in either coral or turquoise coloured beads.

Worked at each end of a suitable piece of ribbon, such ornaments make uncommon-looking and novel book-markers, and as novelties would be certain to sell well at bazaars. An improvement to the appearance of the bead-work, where possible, is to use a larger-sized bead as the seventh, or centre one of each loop, and there are many other ways in which a variety may be made, such, for instance, as the introduction of several shades of colour in the beads, or by the use of beads of a fanciful shape.

No. 25.—KNITTED & BEADED CUFFS.

THESE narrow bands, which resemble bracelets rather than cuffs, are always much appreciated by old ladies, who like to wear them in summer when longer ones are too warm. They may be made in a great variety of colours of beads upon any shade of wool, and can be arranged so as to match any dress. Brown and gold always look well together, so do grey and steel, while metallic beads may now be had in various shades of ruby, peacock blue, bronze, or green, besides the more commonplace gold and silver. The wool may be either single Berlin or Andalusian, the latter by preference, as being softer and more elastic. Knitting silk makes handsome cuffs, but is less pleasant than wool to work with. The beads, of No. 8 size, must be threaded first, and the greater part of them passed along the wool for a long distance before the work is commenced.

Cast on twenty-four stitches, and knit one plain row. Remember that every alternate row must be plain knitting without any beads, or the beads will come on the wrong side of the work. 2nd row—Slip 3 stitches, as if for purling, from the left hand to the right hand needle, pass 4 beads along the wool till they are close to the work, knit 1 stitch. The stitches that are slipped in one row must be very loosely knitted in the next, or the work will be drawn out of place and the cuff rendered too tight. Knit 3 stitches, passing a bead up to each, knit 3, knit 5 stitches with beads, knit 3, knit 3 bead stitches, slip 3, pass along 4 beads. Knit the next row plain. 4th row—Slip 3, pass along 4 beads, knit 1, knit 3 bead stitches, knit 2, slip 1, pass along 4 beads, slip 2, pass along 5 beads, slip 1, pass along 4 beads, knit 2, knit 3 bead stitches, slip 3, pass along 4 beads. Repeat 2nd and 4th rows until the cuff is long enough to fit closely round the wrist. It will probably require about a hundred rows in all. Cast off and sew the ends together on the wrong side.

By casting on about forty-five or fifty stitches and omitting one fringe, the same pattern may be adapted to longer cuffs, and should the bead-work be considered too narrow in proportion to its length, it is easy to add a couple more of the centre loops of slipped beads, remembering to keep the loop in which there are five beads in the middle, and working two loops each with four beads on each side of it. By counting carefully the numbers of beads required, and threading them in rotation, it is quite possible to make the fringe at the edge of one and the middle pattern of a second colour.

No. 26.—BEAD WORK ON CANVAS.

THE vandyke border given here is useful for most purposes to which such a piece of work could be applied when executed in any other style of embroidery, such as mantel borders, valances to brackets, or any similar hangings. Any Berlin woolwork design may be thus reproduced on canvas, each stitch being considered as equivalent to one bead. Geometrical designs work out, as a rule, better than floral ones, and the work is specially to be recommended for anything that is desired to be extremely durable, as it is quite unaffected by climate; neither sunlight, damp, nor London fog injures it in the least, and should the colours of the beads in time become dimmed by dust or smoke, a damp sponge passed carefully over them will soon restore them to their pristine freshness.

The work is most easy and convenient to do when stretched in a frame; each bead is laid on separately, and held with a stitch of strong white thread, which can be waxed if it seems inclined to wear rough as it is pulled through

and through the canvas. Each stitch is taken diagonally across a square of the canvas, thus forming half one of the usual cross-stitches.

The colours of the beads used in this border are nine in number: gold, white of three kinds, chalk, crystal and clouded, black, grey, two shades of blue, and pink. The background may be either filled in with woolwork in the usual way, or may be entirely worked in with beads of a dull neutral tint. Much of the success of the work will depend upon the beads, which must be chosen perfectly symmetrical and regular as to size, shape, and colour, and it is well to bear in mind the indisputable fact that no fancy work of any kind can be good unless it is executed with first-class materials.

It is a pity that this style of work has been allowed to fall into disfavour, for in the hands of any worker possessed of artistic taste it may be made really effective and pleasing. Much of the work done in the olden times by foreigners is worthy of much admiration, but we have hitherto failed dismally, owing to our attempts to portray naturalistic designs with these hard formal materials which although perfectly appropriate for formal patterns, cannot with the slightest success be used to follow the delicate shades and curves of nature.

No. 27.—BEAD MOSAIC.

THIS so-called bead mosaic, thought somewhat tedious to do, especially at first, before one becomes accustomed to it, is extremely useful for making a great many fancy articles. It simply requires as materials, beads all of the same size but of a variety of colours, strong thread, and two small pieces of perforated cardboard. The colours may be varied to suit individual fancy, and any geometrical Berlin woolwork pattern may be thus worked.

For the pattern shown in the wood-cut, twenty pieces of thread are required, each of the length that the beading is to be made. For a wider pattern, of course more threads are required, and the number of these must be always one more than the number of the beads in each row.

Pass the twenty threads through the two pieces of perforated cardboard in the manner shown in the illustration. Knot the ends together at the back of the upper piece of card and pin them firmly down to a weighted cushion. Leave the second piece of cardboard slack so that it will slide up and down, but pin these ends of the thread also down to the cushion. Join the end of a needleful of stout thread to the hole of the card that is nearest to the right-hand thread, thread each bead separately and pass the needle between each alternately, over or under the next thread of the foundation.

No. 27.—Bead Mosaic.

Use the beads in the following sequence:—1st row—1 black, 2 grey, 1 gold, 1 black, 4 grey, 1 black, 4 grey, 1 black, 2 grey, 1 gold, 1 black. 2nd row—1 black, 1 grey, 1 gold, 1 grey, 1 black, 3 grey, 1 red, 1 black, 3 grey, 1 black, 1 grey, 1 gold, 1 grey, 1 black. 3rd row—1 black, 1 gold, 2 grey, 1 black, 2 grey, 1 black, 3 red, 1 black, 2 grey, 1 black, 1 gold, 2 grey, 1 black. 4th row—1 black, 1 grey, 1 gold, 1 grey, 1 black, 3 grey, 1 black, 1 red, 1 black, 3 grey, 1 black, 1 grey, 1 gold, 1 grey, 1 black. 5th row—1 black, 2 grey, 1 gold, 1 black, 4 grey, 1 black, 4 grey, 1 black, 2 grey, 1 gold, 1 black. 6th row—1 black, 1 grey, 1 gold, 1 grey, 1 black, 1 grey, 1 white, 5 grey, 1 white, 1 grey, 1 black, 1 grey, 1 gold, 1 grey, 1 black. 7th row—1 black, 1 gold, 2 grey, 1 black, 2 grey, 2 blue, 1 grey, 2 blue, 2 grey, 1 black, 1 gold, 2 grey, 1 black. 8th row—1 black, 1 grey, 1 gold, 1 grey, 1 black, 2 grey, 2 blue, 1 grey, 2 blue, 2 grey, 1 black, 1 grey, 1 gold, 1 grey, 1 black. 9th row—1 black, 2 grey, 1 gold, 1 black, 4 grey, 1 white, 4 grey, 1 black, 2 grey, 1 gold, 1 black. 10th row—1 black, 1 grey, 1 gold, 1 grey, 1 black, 2 grey, 2 blue, 1 grey, 2 blue, 2 grey, 1 black, 1 grey, 1 gold, 1 grey, 1 black. 11th row—1 black, 1 gold, 2 grey, 1 black, 2 grey, 2 blue, 1 grey, 2 blue, 2 grey, 1 black, 1 gold, 2 grey, 1 black. 12th row—1 black, 1 grey, 1 gold, 1 grey, 1 black, 1 grey, 1 white, 5 grey, 1 white, 1 grey, 1 black, 1 grey, 1 gold, 1 grey, 1 black. Then begin again from the first row.

Such a pattern as the one figured would be useful for table napkin rings, and the initials of the owner may be woven into them very successfully with gold beads, while made about double the width, very handsome bell ropes may be contrived in this way. The beading for these when finished must be laid upon silk, interlined with stiffened muslin and lined with inexpensive silk or sateen. The bead-work will need sewing to its silk foundation along each edge and finally a large brass handle must be added at one end of the bell rope and a hook at the other. Worked with large flat beads, such a design will effectively ornament the back and seat of a folding occasional chair, mixed with plush, or made on a much larger scale can be utilised for mats or urnstands. The work is very strong, and will wear practically for ever. In using large beads it may be necessary to pass the thread through every second or even third hole in the cardboard, so that the beads are placed at the proper distance apart. For making really large pieces of the work, it is a great convenience to stick down the upper strip of perforated cardboard to the edge of a small frame, a frame of a child-slate will answer well. In this case the second piece of cardboard must be left to slide up and down as usual, and the threads twisted round small nails driven into the edge of the frame at regular distances apart.